Aegean

**Recipes from the
Mountains to the Sea**

Marianna Leivaditaki

First published in Great Britain in 2020 by Kyle Books,
an imprint of Octopus Publishing Group Limited
Carmelite House
50 Victoria Embankment
London EC4Y 0DZ

An Hachette UK Company
www.hachette.co.uk

ISBN: 978 085783 807 0

10 9 8 7 6 5 4

Photographer: Elena Heatherwick
Design: Charlotte Heal Design
Food Stylist: Marianna Leivaditaki with Ellie Mulligan
Project Editor: Sophie Allen
Editorial Assistant: Florence Filose
Editorial Director: Judith Hannam
Publisher: Joanna Copestick
Production: Gemma John and Nic Jones

A Cataloguing in Publication record for this title is available from the British Library.

Printed and bound in China

Aegean

Recipes from the Mountains to the Sea

Marianna Leivaditaki

For my mum Nancy; my strongest supporter.
Miss you and love you forever.

Contents

AEGEAN

Introduction

When I was about 17 the only thing I wanted to do was leave Crete. I felt that I had experienced every bit of the island I could possibly want. I felt it had no more to give. I had grown up in a working family where everyone had to contribute in order to maintain the equilibrium. The harmony.

My father is a fisherman and my mother ran the family restaurant by the water. We kids were always on the go; we helped dad with his preparations for a night at sea, helped mum with the cooking and the daytime restaurant chores like the hanging of octopus on our washing line, and then off we went — to the restaurant.

Once there, we would do everything we could. Peel potatoes, gut fish, serve tables — we did it all. It was truly amazing. I remember carrying trays of food to tables that

were literally bigger than me; I must have been around 5 or 6 then. As the night went on and a young person's tiredness kicked in, I would put 2 chairs together, grab a few tablecloths for cover and go to sleep. The chairs became 3 and 4 as I grew older.

That time was truly unforgettable. Even though everyone helped in the family we were also free-spirited children. Running around all day, surrounded by water, heat, real people, and amazing food.

The time came when I was old enough to make decisions for myself and I did go. I searched elsewhere for the adventures I longed for. I went to England and studied, I worked, I then left again to travel and expose myself to more unknowns.

Then I came back. I came back knowing that what I really wanted to do was cook. It was my passion, after all. So I began this journey I am still embarking on and it has been the most amazing experience of my life. Cooking for me is not about owning the extremities of knowledge; it's about feeling it in your stomach, it's about the desire to create, explore and expose yourself in a way that when it works and people feel it, the outcome is simply the fuel to continue.

It's almost 18 years after the time I wanted to leave Crete. One thing I know for sure is that, back then, I was wrong. I don't know whether discovering the island gastronomically has changed my views, but I don't think so. It's simply an incredible place with offerings fit for the Gods.

Sea, mountains, roads that lead to tucked-away hidden villages, people whose passion and stories are worth hours of sitting on a hard chair and sipping raki through to the sunrise. It's a place that only revealed itself to me after I wanted to leave it.

The initial spark that ignited my passion to cook came from there. My childhood years in the small neighbourhood of Halepa were spent mostly in kitchens. All I wanted to do as a child was cook. I would spend hours writing down recipes and watching the amazing ladies create in their kitchens. It fascinated me. I would ask for recipes, write them down carefully, go to the local market, buy my goods and head back home to cook. I was so small I needed a chair to reach the stove. These are the days I remember now, working in a busy London restaurant and loving every moment of it; now I know where it all began.

IN CRETE.

Now, I go back every time I have a spare moment. I get on the plane and I feel what's coming. I smell the salty air before it even touches my face; I taste the food I long to eat before I can even see it. I love going back home.

Being a chef in London, surrounded by amazing people who are doing a similar thing to me day in day out, I have come to respect my heritage and my gastronomic experiences more than ever.

Nowadays, I go back to the island like an explorer. I want to ask all the questions in the world; I want to know the best cheese makers, the perfect olive oil producers, when and what is foraged each season. I want to know everything so I can use it here, in this other country I live in and expose the people who eat the food I cook to new things.

The island has so much to give. And here I am saying the complete opposite to what I thought 18 years ago.

The water gives fish and creatures that you catch and cook simply, the land provides fruit and vegetables that are cooked as main meals and the mountains offer game that is simply an irresistible delicacy.

I want to talk and write about the island and what it has to give. I want to write and document the families that for years have lived in small villages far away from everything and their kitchen tables are the most incredible sights.
I want to photograph the old ladies going out in the heat or the cold and foraging the season's goods. I want to share my experience of being a fisherman's daughter and living a simple but simultaneously so rich life on the island of Crete.

the SEA

Fried Anchovies with Potatoes, Chopped Herbs and Lemon Mayonnaise

Serves 4–6 as a sharing plate

When the moon is big and bright and my dad goes out fishing for larger fish, he uses whole anchovies as bait. (The size of the moon determines which fish you go for and what time of night you set off.) He travels further to find the big fish in the deeper waters that are less disturbed by the moonlight. He says, 'No lights on the boat Marianna – the darker the better – they won't know we are here.' Only the freshest anchovies in the market are purchased for bait and I used to love 'stealing' a few handfuls to deep-fry and eat with lots of lemon juice. The herby potato salad and rich mayonnaise just add to the whole experience.

For the cooked lemon mayonnaise
— 2 whole unwaxed lemons
— 150g (5½oz) sugar
— 1 tbsp sea salt
— 2 tbsp mayonnaise

— 500g (1lb 2oz) Cyprus potatoes, washed, peeled and cut into halves
— 1 small bunch each of parsley, mint and dill, finely chopped
— 300ml (½ pint) extra virgin olive oil
— Juice of 2 lemons
— 500g (1lb 2oz) fresh anchovies, cleaned and kept whole
— Zest of 1 unwaxed lemon
— Zest of 1 unwaxed orange
— Sea salt and freshly ground black pepper, to taste
— Plain flour, for dusting the fish

For the mayonnaise, place the lemons in a small pan with the sugar and salt and cover them with water. Cook over a medium heat for about 40 minutes or until they are really soft. Remove the lemons from the pan, reserving the liquid, cut them in half and discard the pips. Put the lemons with a touch of the liquid in a food processor and blitz until very smooth. It should look similar to a curd. You won't need all of this for this dish, but I always make more than I need as it keeps forever in the fridge.

Put the potatoes in a pan of salted water. Cook over a medium heat until soft but not falling apart, then drain. When cool enough to handle, cut them into discs and place in a bowl.

Season the herbs with salt and toss them in 2 tablespoons of olive oil. Place a pan over a high heat and when it's hot but not smoking, add the herbs and wilt for a minute or two. Remove from the pan and add to the potatoes. Drizzle with olive oil and the lemon juice, then season with salt and pepper.

Meanwhile, heat 200ml (7fl oz) of olive oil in a pan. Put the anchovies in a bowl and season generously with sea salt. Add the lemon and orange zest to the anchovies and dust them in flour. Don't shake them too much – you want a nice thick coating of flour. When the oil is hot, place the anchovies carefully in the pan and fry until golden. Remove using a slotted spoon and transfer onto a plate lined with kitchen paper to absorb any excess oil.

Mix the mayonnaise with 1 tablespoon of the cooked lemon purée and serve alongside the fish and potato salad or, if you prefer, you can mix it in the salad and make it a bit richer.

AEGEAN

Grilled Squid with Graviera, Rocket and Lemon Zest

Serves 4–6 as a sharing plate

It is not very typical to have fish with cheese, but I tried this recipe a while ago and have loved it ever since.

- 4 medium squid (about 600g/1lb 5oz), cleaned, tubes flattened and scored
- 100g (3½oz) Cretan Graviera (or other hard sheep's milk cheese such as Gruyère or Manchego), grated
- Zest and juice of 2 unwaxed lemons
- 1 small bunch of rocket (about 100g/3½oz)
- Sea salt and freshly ground black pepper, to taste

Make sure you season the squid with salt and pepper before cooking. I like to use a charcoal grill to cook the squid as it gives the squid a great flavour. If you are going to use a grill, make sure it's nice and hot, and the charcoal is glowing red. If you don't have a grill, you can pan fry the squid in a very hot pan with a touch of olive oil until it curls up. It shouldn't take more than a minute or two depending on its size.

Using a food processor, blitz the cheese, lemon juice and rocket briefly. Add the lemon zest, season with salt and pepper, pour over the hot squid and eat immediately.

the SEA

Whole Charcoal-grilled Fish with Lemon, Oil and Parsley

— The freshest fish available: mackerel, turbot, sea bass, large sardines, the sole family – gutted and scaled
– Sea salt

For the lemon dressing
— Juice of 4 lemons
— 200ml (7fl oz) extra virgin olive oil
— Sea salt

To serve
— 1 tbsp roughly chopped parsley
— 2 tbsp sea urchin roe, optional

300–500g (10½oz–1lb 2oz) fish per person depending on how much of a feast you are having

I was brought up in a family where the fish we ate would be grilled, fried or made into a soup. There were no sides or sauces other than oil and lemon. To this day, and having eaten amazing fish in restaurants and homes, I still prefer the way I was brought up with. My father believes that when you play around with the fish, it means it's not fresh and you are trying to cover up something. It may be a bit extreme, but the truth is that when the fish is super fresh, it's worth celebrating its flavour.

In our family restaurant, we had a 5-metre charcoal grill. It covered the whole side of one of the walls in the kitchen. The system was simple. My dad's catch would be placed in a box and the customers would come up and choose their fish. The fish would be weighed and brought to the kitchen, then gutted and washed. A 'skara' (grilling basket) would be thrown on the hottest part of the grill to burn – this would stop the skin of the fish sticking to the 'skara' as you want to save the skin because it's tasty and the fish looks better that way. The fish would be salted, cooked on the fire and served with lemon, olive oil and parsley. That's it. Adding sea urchin roe is simply a luxury that makes the dish that bit better.

Season the fish generously with sea salt and place it on a hot 'skara', griddle, rack – whatever it is you are using. Make sure your coals are red hot but not with flames. You want a medium heat. Cook the fish on one side until it's lovely and charred and then turn it to do the same on the other side. Don't keep turning the fish multiple times as on each turn the juices from the fish escape and this will result in a drier fish. Cooking time will obviously depend on the size of the fish: a 200g (7oz) fish will cook in about 8–10 minutes in total whereas a 2kg (4lb 8oz) fish will need 40 minutes to 1 hour. The best way to check whether the fish is ready is to insert a sharp knife into the thickest part of the fish. If the spine has no blood, then it's ready. Overcooking it is also easy, so be aware!

Carefully remove the fish from the grill and place on a platter. Make the dressing by putting the lemon juice, oil and salt into a jar and shaking vigorously. Pour the dressing over the fish and finish with the parsley and sea urchin roe, if you have it. A good salad and fresh bread is all you need to accompany this.

Sea Urchins on Toast

Serves 4

— 6 sea urchins, opened and
   the darker membranes
   between the roes removed
— 4 slices of sourdough,
   toasted
— 1 tbsp extra virgin olive oil
— 2 lemons, halved, for squeezing

In Crete, sea urchins are a delicacy that people enjoy in the simplest way – with olive oil, lemon and fresh bread. Even though they are loved by many, most people have a painful memory of them – I cannot count the times I have stumbled over these amazing creatures, leaving me with numerous long black spikes embedded in the sole of my foot. The pain is horrible and removing the spikes one by one seems impossible at the time. The old people always gave us different advice. As soon as we stepped on them and started screaming, they would send us behind a bush and tell us to wee on the spikes! As strange as it sounds it works – the still-alive spikes die and in a few hours they pop out of the skin with hardly any effort.

Diving for sea urchins is a full-time job in Crete for many families. The diver needs to be equipped with both amazing lungs and knowledge as they need to know which of the different species are best. I was always told to go for the round purple ones with short spikes and not the black ones with long spikes as they are empty. A mask, a knife and usually a pair of gloves is also necessary as they latch on hard to the rocks and even though their removal needs to be gentle, their spikes are there for a reason!

The sea urchins are placed in crates and taken home where usually the whole family joins forces to begin the cleaning. My friend Niko, who collected them for our restaurant, used to empty the crates in the back garden – there were hundreds of them piled up. Back then, a fork was used to open the shell, revealing the bright orange roe that everyone wanted. Nowadays special utensils are available that simply take the top off in one go, but I usually use a pair of scissors to open them. To do this, insert the sharp end of the scissors into the centre of the urchin, where there is almost a little button, and gently break the shell. Carefully follow the circular shape and cut off the lid, revealing the roe. Then, using a teaspoon, gently remove it from the shell, making sure you leave behind any darker matter and membranes. If you want to serve them in their shell, turn them upside down in a bowl of salted water or seawater (washing them with fresh water will destroy their taste) and give them a shake. Unwanted bits should fall out and the roe should stay intact and clean in the shell.

In Crete you usually buy sea urchins cleaned, but you can get them whole in other places. If you are buying them whole, make sure they look alive and active and their spikes are all there. When you smell them, you want to smell the sea. If they smell too strong, don't buy them.

The best way to eat them is raw with olive oil and lemon. Take a piece of fresh bread, place some roe on it and that's it, enjoy. In our restaurant, my brother made an amazing pasta dish with a fresh tomato sauce, chopped parsley and sea urchin roe added at the last moment. It was incredible. Now that I'm away from Crete, I really miss not having urchins all the time. In pure desperation, a few months ago, I arrived at the airport in Chania and drove straight to the fish market to buy a glass of roe. Not being able to wait, I opened the jar in the car and drank the whole thing; no oil, no lemon, no bread, and still the best thing in the world.

Whatever you decide to do with sea urchins, make sure it's simple. They will always be the stars in a dish.

Remove the roe from the shells, following the instructions on the opposite page, and place it on the toast. Drizzle some olive oil, squeeze over lots of lemon juice and heaven has just knocked on your door.

Kakavia – The Fisherman's Soup

Serves 6–8

— 1kg (2lb 4oz) medium potatoes, peeled and cut into quarters
— 1 turbot, about 1.5kg (3lb 5oz), scaled, gutted and cut into 5 pieces, including the head
— 300g (10½oz) red tomatoes, chopped
— A generous amount of sea salt
— 400ml (14fl oz) extra virgin olive oil
— 600ml (20fl oz) water
— Juice of 3 large, juicy lemons

My first memories of eating kakavia are by the sea at Falasarna. Sometimes, in the summer, we would go there and stay in small shacks or we kids would sleep on mattresses in the back of the cars. It was so much fun. We would be free to run around the beach all day and when the sun went down we would play hide and seek for hours. My dad and his friends would go fishing overnight. In the morning, they would return and we would run to their boats to see their catch. The fish that could be sold would be carefully selected and iced immediately in boxes.

Not all the fish would be sold though. There were a lot of little ones that were too small to bother with and others that were just not classed good enough. This is what kakavia is traditionally made of. The fishermen would give bowls of the fish to their wives to clean. The fish would be perfectly prepared by the ladies – our mums.

A large gas hob would be a permanent feature next to the long table that we ate at. An even bigger gas cylinder would be attached to the hob as it's important that you have a strong fire for the soup to be right.

Potatoes would be placed in one single layer to cover the base of the pan. The fish would follow: the large ones first, followed by the small ones on top, a couple of chopped ripe tomatoes, lots of sea salt and then olive oil and water.

Kakavia takes a lot of olive oil, which is why it turns into this amazing golden silky soup. For every 2½ glasses of water, you put in 1 glass of olive oil. The liquid must just cover the fish – but not fully – too much liquid and it won't be rich enough, too little and there won't be enough for everyone to eat.

The hob would be set alight and the pot would start bubbling. My dad used to say that you must never stir kakavia, just shake the pot, which I was allowed to do sometimes.

Meanwhile, we would be asked to squeeze lemon juice. After a lot of pot shakes and a while of hard boiling, the soup would be ready. The lemon juice would be poured in the pot and the gas hob turned off.

Kakavia needs to rest. In the meantime, the table would be set with shallow soup bowls. A basket full of Cretan barley rusks would be in the centre. The pot would be brought to the table, the fish carefully taken out and put onto a platter and the soup shared between our bowls. Sometimes we didn't use spoons – we crushed the rusks into our bowls, let them soak up some of the soup and picked them up with our fingers.

The leaves from the salty tamarisk trees would fall into our bowls and every time I used to try and remove them, my dad's best friend, Haralambos, would say, 'Eee Marianna, what are you doing? It's seasoning!'

Since then, I have seen kakavia being made and have made it myself hundreds of times. It took many years before I was trusted to make it for customers at our family restaurant. But what is still so special about making it is that every time the excitement and nervousness is the same as the first time. Making a good kakavia means making a lot of people happy around a table – at least in my house! Turbot works beautifully, but if it's not available, gurnard, hake or halibut will also make a delicious soup. It is important that you include the head of the fish in your soup even if you don't fancy eating it. It's the gelatine in the fish and the good olive oil that turn this soup into a silky thick broth that you will never want to end.

Use a saucepan that will fit the potatoes snugly in a single layer at the bottom of the pan. Add the potatoes and then the fish, followed by the tomatoes, salt, extra virgin olive oil and water. The liquid will partly cover the fish, but not entirely. Place the saucepan over a high heat and bring to the boil, cover with a lid and continue to boil for 20 minutes. Shake the pan every so often, but never stir the contents. Before you turn the soup off, make sure that the potatoes are soft. Add the lemon juice, give the pan a final shake and let it sit for 15 minutes before serving.

To serve, use a slotted spoon to very carefully remove the fish to a platter. Divide the soup and potatoes into bowls. In Crete, we serve this soup with barley rusks but lovely toasted sourdough will work perfectly too.

Sun-dried Octopus

Serves 4–6 as a sharing plate

This is not a recipe as such, it is a ritual. It's engrained deeply in my childhood memories and when the charcoal is going and the sun is hot, it must be done.

Most people use washing lines to hang out wet clothes. This was not the case in our house. Our washing line was used for hanging clothes too, but mostly it served another purpose – the hanging of the octopus. Every day, at around 1pm, the ritual would take place. The octopus was brought home from the fish market, placed in the old marble sink in the kitchen and prepared.

First you slit the hood open so it is flat, then you make another slit from the base of the hood to the mouth (beak), remove it and then cut in between two of the legs, just under the slit you have made, so that the whole octopus is flat. You put all the octopus in a large bucket – we prepared about 30 a day – and take it to the washing line. Each octopus needs four pegs. Two for the hood, and two for the first two legs on either side of the hood. We would let it hang for 4–5 hours under the hot sun. (I have never really understood why bees love octopus so much. They would gather in great numbers and feast for hours. When it was time to remove the octopus from the line, it was terrifying, but the octopus would be stiff and dry – perfect for what was going to happen next.)

When the charcoal was lit and the coals were red hot, but without flames, we would place each octopus on a 'skara' (grilling basket) and grill it for about 30–40 minutes, turning it every so often so it didn't burn. When it was cooked, we simply served it with a quarter of a lemon and that was it.

A glass of ouzo with lots of ice or a small glass of Cretan raki matches this delicacy perfectly.

All you need is a charcoal grill, an octopus weighing approximately 1kg (2lb 4oz) or more and lemons.

AEGEAN

Octopus with Red Wine and Black Olive Pasta

Serves 4–6 as a sharing plate

There is a small taverna in Chania by the sea in Nea Hora that does the best red wine octopus. Cooked slowly with red wine and olive oil, the sauce thickens and becomes incredibly tasty – so good to dip fresh bread into. They serve it as it is in a small plate as a mezze; the addition of pasta here is great and the black olives complement this dish enormously. If you don't have time or don't want to make your own pasta you can use a small pasta like ditalini or macaroni and add a few chopped black olives to the dish while cooking.

For the black olive pasta
- 45g (1¾oz) pitted Kalamata olives
- 1 tsp sea salt
- 4 tbsp water
- 2 large organic eggs
- 400g (14oz) pasta flour (type 00)

- 1 double sucker octopus (usually found frozen), around 1–1.2kg (2lb 4oz–2lb 8oz)
- 150ml (¼ pint) extra virgin olive oil
- 300ml (½ pint) good-quality red wine
- 2 garlic cloves, peeled and chopped
- 6 bay leaves
- 800g (1lb 12oz) ripe red tomatoes, blitzed
- Sea salt, to taste

This dough can be made a day in advance and stored in the fridge if preferable. Put the olives, salt and water into a food processor and pulse to a fine paste. If necessary, add one of the eggs to the processor to help get a smooth consistency. At this point, you have two options: you can either make the pasta dough by hand or you can use a food processor. This really depends on you. Both ways work perfectly.

If you have a food processor that is large enough, add the egg(s) and flour to the food processor with the olive paste and pulse until the mixture just starts to come together – it will begin to resemble a rough crumble. Tip the ingredients from the food processor onto a work surface and knead the dough for around 10 minutes until it springs back when pressed with a finger. If the dough is too stiff, you can wet your hands to gently hydrate the dough as you knead. Try to refrain from adding more flour once you begin kneading – as the gluten develops the dough will become less sticky. Form the dough into a ball, slightly flatten and flour it and place in a bowl with a damp towel resting on top – let it rest for at least 30 minutes.

If you are going to make the pasta traditionally, put the flour on a work surface and make a well in the centre. Add the eggs and olive paste to the middle of the well and, with a fork, begin to whisk the egg and olive mixture to aerate it. After a minute or so, gradually begin to incorporate the flour mixture from the rim of the well into the eggy olive mixture. Continue to add the flour mixture a bit at a time until it becomes difficult to move the mixture around with the fork. With your hands, push the remaining flour onto the eggy mixture and begin to knead the dough for around 10 minutes until the dough springs back when pressed with a finger. If the dough is too stiff, you can wet your hands to gently hydrate the dough as you knead.

If you are going to roll this out by hand, I would suggest dividing the dough into two smaller balls before resting. If using a pasta machine, I would suggest rolling out a quarter of the dough at a time. I would aim for the second smallest setting on your typical home machine.

I prefer rolling it out by hand and you don't have to go extra thin with this recipe. I would suggest rolling it on a lightly floured surface as thin as you can go. Cut it into squares (2cm/¾in) and place it on a dry cloth to dry out until needed.

The 'hood' of the octopus refers to the head – the pouch-like part to which all the legs are attached. Slice it open to create a flat hood that will show the beak at the centre, which should be removed. Continue to slice to separate the two legs under the initial incision to make the octopus look flat.

Heat a saucepan large enough to easily fit the octopus over a high heat. When the pan is really hot, add the octopus and don't worry that it will burn. An octopus contains a large amount of water and you don't need to add extra water. Give it a few minutes and you will see that your pan will have a fair amount of liquid in it – don't worry either about all the sounds that the liquid makes. Cook for about 10 minutes over a medium heat. At this point the colour of the octopus will have changed to a redder shade and it will have started to shrink. Add the olive oil and red wine to the pan together with the garlic and bay leaves and continue to cook for another 10 minutes. Add the tomatoes, place a lid on the pan and reduce the heat to low. Cook for about 30 minutes or until the octopus is tender and the sauce has thickened.

Remove the octopus from the pan, place on a board and cut into small, bite-sized pieces. Add the pasta to the pan and cook for a few minutes until ready. You should have enough sauce in the pan to cook the pasta. However, if you feel there is not enough sauce, feel free to add a splash of water. Be aware though that this dish is thick and rich. Return the octopus to the pan and give everything a final stir. Season and serve. We wait until right at the end to add salt as octopus is naturally quite salty, so refrain from doing this sooner as you may find you don't need any extra.

Tarama with Smoked Fish, 'Ash' Potatoes and Crunchy Vegetables

Serves 4

These potatoes are not cooked in ash, but they taste as if they have been in a way. If you prefer to cook them in ash, wrap them in foil and bury them in the barbecue under hot ash (a more detailed explanation can be found on page 40). Here I use the hob and a pot – this is a method I learned working at Moro. They're a typical dish of the Canary Islands, where they are called 'papas arrugadas' (wrinkled potatoes), and are traditionally cooked in sea water.

For the tarama
— 120g (4½oz) smoked cod's roe, roughly chopped
— 100g (3½oz) sourdough bread, crusts removed
— Juice of 2 lemons
— 5 tbsp extra virgin olive oil
— 2 tbsp double cream
— 50ml (2fl oz) water
— Zest and juice of ½ unwaxed orange
— 1 tsp black pepper, coarsely ground
— paprika, to garnish

— 500g (1lb 2oz) baby potatoes
— 1 tbsp sea salt
— Carrots, radishes, kohlrabi, cucumbers, cut into strips or whatever shape you like to dip into the tarama

Make the tarama by blitzing all the ingredients in a food processor until creamy and very smooth. Check the flavour as you may need to adjust the seasoning depending on how salty the roe is. Place in the fridge until needed.

Put the potatoes in a single layer in a pan and add enough water to just cover them. Add the salt and use a sheet of baking parchment (not a lid) to cover them. Allow them to cook over a medium heat for about 20–25 minutes. At this point the water will have evaporated and the potatoes will begin to wrinkle and shrivel a bit. You need to wait until the potatoes are completely dry and there is zero moisture left. They will begin to stick to the base of the pan so you will need to shake them frequently to stop them from burning. When they are ready, they will be delicious and soft.

Garnish the tarama with paprika and olive oil, and serve with the potatoes and the raw vegetables and enjoy at home or as a seaside picnic snack.

Pan-fried Prawns with Metaxa

Serves 4–6 as a sharing plate

This is an excellent dish for real seafood lovers who have no fear of tucking into whole prawns and no hesitation when it comes to sucking all the lovely juices from their shells. My only advice is: don't be shy, but you may want to consider finger bowls.

- 100g (3½oz) salted butter
- 1 tsp grated fresh ginger
- 500g (1lb 2oz) fresh whole prawns, shells on
- 4 tbsp metaxa (Greek brandy), or another good-quality brandy
- Juice of 1 lemon
- 1 handful of fresh parsley, roughly chopped
- Sea salt and freshly ground black pepper, to taste

Heat a large pan over a medium heat and add the butter and the grated ginger. When the butter begins to take a light golden colour, add the prawns and turn the heat to high. Toss the prawns in the butter by shaking the pan until they turn a shade of pink, which means they are ready. Add the brandy, lemon juice, season with salt and pepper and give the pan a final shake. Remove from the heat, transfer to a plate together with all the juices and sprinkle over some freshly chopped parsley.

AEGEAN

Prawns with Ouzo, Orzo and Courgette

Serves 4

This dish is delicate and velvety and it's perfect in the summer when the courgettes are at their best. Make sure you get fresh prawns for this and their size is irrelevant as long as they are so fresh that they are almost still alive. Pick small tender and firm courgettes and if they happen to have flowers attached to them then add these too.

— 400g (14oz) fresh prawns,
  peeled, shells reserved

For the prawn stock
— 1 tbsp extra virgin olive oil
— 1 fennel bulb, roughly chopped
— 1 celery stick, roughly chopped
— 1 red pepper, roughly chopped
— 1 white onion, roughly chopped
— 3 bay leaves
— A pinch of saffron
— 200ml (7fl oz) white wine
— 50ml (2fl oz) brandy

— 1 tbsp good-quality butter
— 200g (7oz) orzo pasta
— 3 pale green courgettes,
  very thinly sliced
— 500g (1lb 2oz) cherry tomatoes,
  quartered
— 1 tbsp extra virgin olive oil
— ½ tsp crushed fennel seeds
— 20ml (4 tsp) Greek ouzo
— Zest of 1 lemon
— Zest of 1 orange
— 1 handful of mint leaves,
  chopped

Preheat the oven to 180°C/350°F/gas mark 4.

Place the prawn shells on a baking tray and dry out in the oven for about 20–30 minutes. This really helps to concentrate and increase the flavour of the shells.

Heat the oil in a pan and add all the stock ingredients. Toss around and cook gently for 10 minutes with no water. You want to caramelize and sweeten the vegetables. Add the prawn shells to the pan and cover with water. Simmer gently for 30 minutes. Turn the heat off and allow the stock to rest for a while before passing it through a sieve and reserving the liquid.

Heat the butter in a pan and add the orzo. Stir gently for a couple of minutes until it's all shiny and coated in the butter. Add half the courgettes and all the tomatoes together with the oil and fennel seeds. Increase the heat and start adding the prawn stock in batches – you may not need to use all of it. The orzo will take about 15 minutes to cook. Just before it's ready, add the remaining courgettes, ouzo and lemon and orange zest. Finally add the prawns and check the seasoning. Cook until the prawns turn pink. You want this dish to be loose and juicy – a bit like a risotto. Serve with the fresh mint scattered over the top.

If you have any prawn stock left over, freeze it to use another time.

Baked Potatoes Stuffed with Prawns and Smoked Salmon Mayonnaise

Serves 4

- 4 medium potatoes, washed and stabbed with a sharp-pointed knife
- 200g (7oz) fresh prawns, heads and tails removed
- 2 baby gem lettuce, sliced thinly
- 1 tbsp chopped tarragon
- 4 tbsp lemony aioli (see page 71)
- 1 tbsp very finely chopped smoked salmon
- Juice of 2 lemons
- 1 tbsp extra virgin olive oil
- Sea salt and freshly ground black pepper, to taste

I had to include this dish in this collection. It was my mum's creation at the restaurant and it was so popular that sometimes more than half of the enormous charcoal grill was taken over by potatoes buried under hot ash. Looking for them was tricky business and a potato detector was a gadget we all wished we had.

We would sit on the cement steps with a large sack of potatoes in front of us. This was a job given to me from a very young age and without a doubt the sack of potatoes must have been three times my weight. I had to be careful not to tilt it too much in my searches for the perfect potato as I would never be able to pick it up again and we would end up with a floor full of loose muddy potatoes.

After the potatoes were chosen, I would use my half-broken bright green 'potato bucket', which, because it had holes, wasn't good for anything else, to make a few trips to the sink and back until they were all delivered. I would wash them under cold water and use a metal brush to get rid of all the mud stuck to them. Then, with a pointed knife, I would stab them a few times in various places and wrap them in kitchen foil.

On busy nights we had to cook more than 30 of them. I used to take them to the charcoal grill before it was lit and very carefully dig a hole (or more like a whole area) in which I could bury them. After the charcoal was lit on the opposite side of the grill, I would take the lovely hot coals and spread them on the base of the hole I had dug. I would cover these with a thick layer of ash, then place the potatoes on top of it, followed by another layer of ash, more hot coals and finished with ash again. We used to cook them for about an hour and a half.

When ready, we would unwrap them and the smell was incredible. I very often had them with olive oil, oregano, lemon juice and salt. The best and the simplest snack ever. At the restaurant we used to serve them with prawns, mayonnaise and baby gem and the Greeks, most of whom had probably never seen a stuffed potato before, ended up loving Nancy's version of a baked potato.

If you have a charcoal grill and feel adventurous, go ahead and cook them in the ash. However, they come out almost as nice baked in the oven.

Preheat the oven to 220°C/425°F/gas mark 7. Wrap the potatoes in kitchen foil and place in the oven for about 1 hour or until they are soft and ready.

Blanch the prawns in salted water for 1–2 minutes depending on size, remove them from the pot and peel them. Put the prawns in a bowl with all the remaining ingredients, give them a good stir and adjust the seasoning. Cut the potatoes open lengthways and add the filling to the middle. Eat straight away.

Spicy Summer Salad with Clams and Crispy Capers

Serves 4–6 as a sharing plate

This is a very fresh and delicious way to eat clams – all salty, juicy and tangy. It's the best salad to have on a hot summer's day with some fried fish and a nice cold beer. Make sure the clams are super fresh and alive and that's all you need really.

- 1kg (2lb 4oz) palourde clams
- 4 tbsp capers
- 100ml (3½fl oz) sunflower oil (or a similar light frying oil)
- 3 tbsp extra virgin olive oil
- 1 green horn pepper
- 1 red horn pepper
- 2 large ripe red tomatoes
- 1 crisp cucumber
- 2 green chillies
- 1 red chilli
- 1 handful of parsley
- 1 handful of coriander
- Juice of 2–3 lemons depending on size
- Sea salt, to taste

Place the clams in a bowl of ice-cold water for about 1 hour to remove any sand trapped inside them.

Pat dry the capers on some kitchen paper. Heat the sunflower oil in a small pan and, when hot, add the capers and fry until crispy. When they start shrivelling and go slightly darker, remove them with a slotted spoon and scatter them on kitchen paper to remove excess oil and crisp up. Don't wait for them to darken in colour before you remove them as they will taste burnt. Put to one side.

Use your hands to pick the clams out of the water so that the collected sand stays in the bottom of the bowl.

Heat a large pan over a medium heat. When hot, add the clams and 1 tablespoon of olive oil. Cover the pan with a lid and wait for the clams to just open. This should take about 2 minutes. Remove the clam shells from the heat and pass the liquid through a sieve. Put to one side. Take the clams out of their shells and reserve them, with their liquid.

Chop all the vegetables and herbs as small as possible – as if you are almost making a salsa. Don't squash them, just go as small as possible.

Put the vegetables and herbs in a bowl with the clams and their liquid and add the lemon juice, the remaining oil and salt to taste. You can add more or less lemon juice according to taste. I prefer it very tangy and quite salty. Place the bowl in the fridge as the salad is much better when served chilled. Just before you serve, add the crispy capers on top.

I like to serve this in bowls with spoons. It will also keep perfectly in the fridge for another day.

Fresh Prawn Omelette with Coriander and Chilli Sauce

— 1 tbsp extra virgin olive oil

— 1 Turkish green pepper, chopped

— 6 organic eggs

— 300g (10½oz) fresh prawns, shelled

— 3 tbsp double cream

— 1 tsp black pepper

— 1 tbsp tarragon leaves, chopped

— 1 tbsp butter, soft

— 1 small handful of fresh coriander leaves, chopped

For the chilli sauce

— 500g (1lb 2oz) red chillies, deseeded and roughly chopped

— 400g (14oz) ripe tomatoes, chopped

— 200g (7oz) sugar

— 1 tsp ground coriander seeds

— 1 tsp smoked sweet paprika

— Sea salt, to taste

Serves 4–6 as a sharing plate

My mum used to make this omelette in our restaurant and the customers loved it. She made it plump and fluffy and, every time one was ordered, we all asked for another one for us to share. She didn't use coriander or chilli sauce, but both go incredibly well with this. You can use whatever prawns you like for this dish as long as they are fresh. It makes all the difference.

The chilli sauce recipe will give you more sauce than you need, but it's really not worth making this in smaller quantities. I would actually double the recipe to make a nice big batch. It keeps really well for about a week in the fridge.

To make the chilli sauce, place all the ingredients in a pan, cover and cook gently for 20–25 minutes. Everything should be soft and glossy by this time.

Allow to cool for a while and blitz using a food processor. If you prefer the sauce to be chunkier, leave out this step.

Heat the pan that you are going to make the omelette in – it can be 20cm (8in) in diameter or smaller if you prefer a thick omelette. Add the olive oil and green pepper to the pan and fry gently for a few minutes until soft.

Crack the eggs into a bowl and give them a quick whisk with a fork. Add the prawns, cream, pepper, tarragon and butter to the bowl and mix.

Pour the mix into the pan over the peppers and lower the heat. When the omelette is lovely and golden on the bottom you can either flip it using a plate or place it under the grill for a minute or two until the top is cooked and golden too.

If you are going to flip it with a plate, make sure the pan is oiled and clean when you return the omelette. When ready, serve with chopped fresh coriander on top and the chilli sauce on the side.

This must be eaten hot and I love to eat it with crispy baby gem lettuce cut into quarters.

Stuffed Cuttlefish or Squid with Sun-dried Tomatoes, Anchovies, Goat's Curd and Sage

Serves 4–6 as a sharing plate

Having left Crete to study in England, I found myself back there again after travelling through Europe and South America. I took over the kitchen at my parents' restaurant and felt passionate about making it a more creative menu. This is one of the dishes I came up with and was very happy with. Knowing that our very 'palate-conservative' customers would never order it, I started sending it to tables for free. 'On the house', I would say, 'Just try it and let me know'. It quickly became very popular.

Both cuttlefish and squid are perfect for this recipe, so just choose the freshest one you can find. Ask your fishmonger to clean cuttlefish for you.

For the stuffing
— 4 tbsp finely chopped sun-dried tomatoes
— 10 anchovy fillets, chopped
— 300g (10½oz) goat's curd
— 4 tbsp finely chopped mint leaves
— 300g (10½oz) chard, finely chopped, plus 2 whole large chard leaves for the baking tray
— 2 tbsp finely chopped sage leaves
— 1 tbsp capers
— Sea salt and freshly ground black pepper, to taste

— 600–800g (1lb 5oz–1lb 12oz) fresh cuttlefish or squid, cleaned but kept whole
— 5 tbsp extra virgin olive oil, plus extra to serve
— A handful of rocket leaves
— Juice of ½ lemon

Preheat the oven to 180ºC/350ºF/gas mark 4.

Place all the stuffing ingredients in a bowl together with 3 tablespoons of the olive oil and mix well. Stuff the cuttlefish or squid with the mix. If using squid, use the tentacles to close the opening at the top. If using cuttlefish, you don't need to close the opening.

Place the whole chard leaves on the base of a small baking tray and add the stuffed cuttlefish or squid. Drizzle with the remaining olive oil and sprinkle a touch of extra salt over the top. Cover with baking parchment and place in the oven for 30–40 minutes or until tender. Remove the parchment and place the tray under a hot grill long enough to get some colour.

Remove from the grill and serve whole or cut into smaller pieces. Serve with some rocket leaves, seasoned with lemon juice, olive oil and salt.

the SEA

Fried Salt Cod with Beetroot and Garlic Mash

Serves 4

Deep-fried salt cod in batter is quite common in Greece and usually served with 'skordalia', a potato and garlic or sometimes bread and garlic dip. It's strong and potent because of the enormous amount of garlic in the sauce but so good it's irresistible. Usually a bunch of parsley is passed around the table to chew on after eating in order to enable conversation with others who have not had the same lunch as you.

This version with beetroot is lighter and less heavy and the addition of walnuts makes it very tasty.

— 300g (10½oz) salt cod, soaked overnight in lots of water
— 100g (3½oz) plain flour
— ½ can of beer (approximately)
— 2 beetroots
— 1 slice of sourdough bread
— 4 garlic cloves, crushed
— 1 small handful of walnuts
— 2 tsp good-quality red wine vinegar
— 2 tbsp extra virgin olive oil
— 300ml (½ pint) vegetable oil, for frying
— Sea salt, to taste

Put the cod in a bowl big enough so that you can cover the cod with water. Before you leave the cod to soak overnight, make sure you change the water a few times.

The following day, cut the cod into bite-sized pieces and put to one side. Make sure you check how salty it is. It will obviously be a bit salty, but you don't want the salt to be overpowering.

Whisk the flour with enough beer to create a batter that resembles thick double cream. Let it sit in the fridge until needed.

Boil the beetroot in a pan of water until soft. Remove from the water, peel and chop roughly. Using a food processor, blitz the beetroot together with the bread, garlic, walnuts, vinegar and olive oil until smooth. Season the mash with salt.

Heat the oil in a frying pan until hot but not smoking. (Test the oil by adding a small piece of cod and if it bubbles instantly then it's good to go.) Drop the cod bites into the batter then into the hot oil. Cook until crispy and golden all round. Remove from the oil using a slotted spoon and place on kitchen paper to absorb excess oil.

Serve hot with the beetroot and garlic mash.

AEGEAN

Black Orzo with Cuttlefish and Green Peas

Serves 6–8 as a sharing plate

When I was growing up in Crete, the only thing we would cook orzo with was lamb baked in the oven. These days it is used a lot by less traditional chefs instead of rice and it works really well. A cuttlefish and ink stew is amazing without rice or pasta, but a bit of orzo does make it delicious and texturally more interesting.

For the cuttlefish
— 700–800g (1lb 9oz–1lb 12oz) fresh whole cuttlefish, cleaned and cut into bite-sized pieces
— 200ml (7fl oz) white wine
— 50ml (2fl oz) extra virgin olive oil
— Zest of 1 lemon
— 5 bay leaves
— 100ml (3½fl oz) water

For the orzo
— 3 tbsp extra virgin olive oil
— 2 garlic cloves, chopped
— 2 red horn peppers, finely chopped
— 1 fennel bulb, finely chopped
— 1 red onion, diced
— 1 carrot, coarsely grated
— 5 thyme sprigs, picked and stems discarded
— ⅓ Scotch bonnet chilli, chopped
— 150g (5½oz) orzo pasta
— 1 tbsp cuttlefish ink or about 8 small sachets
— 1kg (2lb 4oz) fresh peas, podded (or 200g/7oz frozen peas)
— 4–5 basil leaves, shredded by hand
— Zest and juice of 1 lemon

Place the cuttlefish in a pan with the wine, oil, lemon zest, bay leaves and water and cook gently for about 30 minutes or until it is soft. Remove from the pan using a slotted spoon and allow to cool down. Pass the cooking liquid through a sieve and reserve for later.

Start cooking the orzo base by heating the olive oil in a pan and browning the garlic. Add the peppers, fennel, onion and carrot together with the thyme and chilli. Cook over a medium heat for about 20 minutes until the vegetables are soft and sweet. Add the orzo, cuttlefish, cuttlefish ink, peas and the reserved cooking liquid. Stir often to make sure the orzo does not stick to the bottom of the pan – it should take about 15–20 minutes to cook. This dish is meant to be juicy, so if you feel you need to add a touch of water or wine go ahead. When ready, turn the heat off and add the basil, lemon zest and juice. Adjust the seasoning and serve immediately.

Cod and Clams with Smoked Spicy Gazpacho and Bread Salad

Serves 4, or 8 as a sharing plate

This dish may sound a bit elaborate but it's not that complicated to make. The end result is so good that I could not resist including it in this collection. Make sure you use sustainably sourced cod.

— 4 cod fillets (700–800g/
   1lb 9oz–1lb 12oz)
— 400g (14oz) clams, kept in ice-
   cold water for 1 hour (this helps
   clean out any trapped sand)
— 1 tbsp extra virgin olive oil
— 100ml (3½fl oz) good-quality
   white wine
— Sea salt and freshly ground black
   pepper, to taste

For the smoked spicy gazpacho
— 250g (9oz) ripe red tomatoes
— 1 red romano pepper, deseeded
— 1 small red onion, peeled
— 1 red chilli, deseeded
— 1 tsp Turkish chilli flakes
— 1 medium slice of sourdough
— 1 tbsp quality red wine vinegar
— 100ml (3½fl oz) extra virgin
   olive oil
— Sea salt, to taste

For the cod's roe butter
— 4 tbsp butter
— 1 tsp Turkish chilli flakes
— 50g (1¾oz) smoked cod's roe,
   chopped

For the bread salad
— 2 medium slices of sourdough
— 50g (1¾oz) black olives, pitted
— 200g (7oz) samphire
— 50ml (2fl oz) extra virgin olive oil
— 1 tbsp quality red wine vinegar
— Zest of 1 unwaxed lemon

To make the gazpacho, put the tomatoes, pepper, onion, chilli and chilli flakes in a food processor and blitz vigorously for a minute or two. Pass the ingredients through a fine sieve and return the strained juice to the food processor. Add the bread, vinegar and salt and blitz again. Using the opening at the top, start adding the olive oil nice and slowly as if you were making mayonnaise. You will see the mixture lightening in colour and thickening as it emulsifies. Adjust the seasoning as desired. Place in a jug and put in the fridge until needed.

To make the cod's roe butter, melt the butter in a small pan over a medium heat. When it begins to turn golden, add the chilli flakes and give it a stir for another 10 seconds. Add the chopped roe, remove from the heat and leave to one side, preferably somewhere warm but not hot.

To make the bread salad, preheat the oven to 160°C/325°F/gas mark 3. Cut the bread into small cubes, place on a baking tray and bake until golden brown. Remove from the oven and place in a bowl. Mix the bread with all the other ingredients and put to one side. You don't want the salad to sit around for too long as it will get soggy, but a bit of time is good for the ingredients to mingle.

When you are ready to serve, cook the fish and clams. Heat a pan over a medium heat. Season the cod with salt and pepper and coat it with the olive oil. Place in the hot pan and cook until one side is golden. Flip the fish to cook the other side and add the clams together with the wine. Place a lid over the pan and cook until the fish is cooked and the clams have just opened (about 2 minutes).

To serve, put some gazpacho on a plate, or platter if you are sharing, and place the fish and clams on top. Scatter the salad all over and finish with the cod's roe butter.

AEGEAN

Mussel Saganaki with Feta, Fennel and Ouzo

Serves 4–6 as a sharing plate

Another staple from our family restaurant in Crete. In the summer months when we were super busy, part of the prep would be to clean, cook and shell 20kg (more than 40lb) of mussels just for this dish. I simply love it.

Heat a medium saucepan over a medium heat. When hot, add the olive oil followed by the peppers, onion, fennel, garlic, chillies and anise seeds. Season with salt and pepper, turn down the heat and place a lid on the pan. Cook for about 20–30 minutes or until everything becomes sweet and golden.

Meanwhile, heat another pan over a high heat and add the mussels and wine. Cook until the mussels have just opened. Remove their shells and put the mussels to one side. Keep the cooking liquid, as you may need it later to thin the sauce down a bit.

Add the ouzo and feta to the pepper and onion base and stir gently until the feta begins to melt. This should only take a couple of minutes. Add the mussels and turn off the heat.

Sprinkle over some chopped parsley and serve with freshly toasted bread.

- 4 tbsp extra virgin olive oil
- 1 red horn pepper, finely chopped
- 1 green bell pepper, finely chopped
- 1 medium white onion, finely chopped
- 1 fennel bulb, finely chopped
- 3 garlic cloves, chopped
- 3 red fresh chillies, cut lengthways, deseeded and chopped
- 1 tsp crushed green anise seeds
- 1kg (2lb 4oz) fresh mussels
- 200ml (7fl oz) white wine
- 3 tbsp ouzo
- 200g (7oz) good-quality feta, crumbled
- 1 handful of fresh parsley, chopped
- Sea salt and freshly ground black pepper, to taste

the SEA

Fried Sardines with Courgette, Tahini and Pumpkin Seed Salad

Serves 6–8 as a sharing plate

Sardines and tahini for some reason seem to be a good pairing. I love adding tender fresh courgettes to this salad because their delicacy can really take the tahini and lemon sauce to a nicer place. I love the combination of the creaminess of the dressed courgettes together with the crispiness of the sardines.

- 2–3 medium courgettes, sliced as thinly as possible
- 3 tbsp extra virgin olive oil
- 1 garlic clove, finely chopped
- 200ml (7fl oz) olive oil or a good vegetable oil, for frying
- 500g (1lb 2oz) sardines, scaled, gutted and filleted
- 100g (3½oz) plain flour
- 1 tbsp pumpkin seeds
- 2 tsp tahini
- Juice of 1 lemon
- Sea salt, to taste
- Lemon wedges, to serve

You can slice the courgettes with a sharp knife or with a mandolin if you have one. Sprinkle some salt over them and let them sit for 5 minutes.

Heat a pan over a medium heat and, when hot, add 2 tablespoons of extra virgin olive oil followed by the chopped garlic. When the garlic turns golden, add the courgettes and turn up the heat to high.

Toss the courgettes for a few minutes until they are just cooked. You want them to have a nice texture rather than turn mushy. Remove them from the heat and put to one side.

Heat the oil to fry the fish until hot but not smoking. (You can test it by sprinkling some flour into the oil, which should bubble instantly if it's ready.) Season the sardine fillets with salt and dust with flour. Lower into the hot oil and cook on both sides until golden and crispy. Remove from the oil and place on kitchen paper to absorb the excess oil.

Put the courgettes in a bowl and add the pumpkin seeds, tahini, the remaining tablespoon of extra virgin olive oil, lemon juice and salt. They should look creamy and delicious. Place on a plate and add the fried sardines over the top. Serve with extra lemon wedges.

the SEA

Stuffed Grilled Mackerel in Vine Leaves with Purslane, Tomato and Yogurt Salad

— 4 tbsp pine nuts
— 4 tsp raisins
— 1 tsp chopped marjoram
— 1 tsp dried oregano
— 1 tbsp extra virgin olive oil, plus a little extra if grilling in the oven
— Juice of 1 lemon
— 4 medium mackerel (approximately 1kg/2lb 4oz), gutted and cleaned
— 12 preserved vine leaves
— Sea salt and freshly ground black pepper, to taste

For the salad
— 1 bunch of purslane, roughly chopped
— 2 medium ripe tomatoes, roughly chopped
— 2 tsp tahini
— 1 tbsp extra virgin olive oil
— Juice of 1 lemon
— Sea salt and freshly ground black pepper, to taste

Serves 4, or 8 as a sharing plate

As kids we used to pick the tender swirly shoots from the vines in late spring and chew on them for hours. They were really sour and made us shiver briefly. We collected the leaves, washed them and used them for stuffing. When we had more than we needed, the ladies would preserve them by bundling them up, rolling them and placing them in jars. They added salt and water to the jars and boiled them briefly until their colour started to change. They would then remove them from the hot water, turn the jars upside down and let them cool. This would get rid of excess air in the jars that would disrupt their preservation.

I can still picture dozens of upside-down jars on the table under the almond tree. How satisfying that must have been to know that they now had vine leaves to use all year round.

I use them in many ways. Of course I love them stuffed, but I also like to use them as a base on a plate with cured fish, chop them up in stews or wrap fish in them, as I do here.

Put the pine nuts, raisins, marjoram, oregano, oil and lemon juice in a food processor and blitz roughly. Stuff the bellies of the fish with this mixture. To wrap the fish in the leaves, open 3 leaves on a board side by side, overlapping them a little so there are no gaps. Place a fish in the middle and wrap it with the vine leaves. Do the same for the rest.

Make the salad by adding all the ingredients to a bowl and mixing by hand. You want some of those tomato juices to escape and become part of the dressing. Adjust the seasoning and place the bowl in the fridge.

If you have a charcoal grill going, that is the best way to cook the fish. However, the grill setting in your oven will make them delicious too. If you are using your oven, line a tray with baking parchment and place the fish on it. Season generously with sea salt and a touch of olive oil. You won't need the oil if you are using a charcoal grill. Cook the fish on one side, making sure the leaves start colouring and charring, then flip and cook on the other side. They will need about 5–6 minutes per side. To check if they are ready, insert a knife at the thickest point of the fish spine and make sure there is no blood.

Scatter the salad all over the fish and serve.

the SEA

Ouzo-cured Trout with Fennel and Red Onion Salad

- 1 trout fillet (about 400g/14oz), boned
- 200g (7oz) fine sea salt
- 200g (7oz) caster sugar
- 50ml (2fl oz) Greek ouzo
- 100ml (3½fl oz) fresh beetroot juice, collected by grating and squeezing 4–6 fresh beetroot
- 1 tsp fennel seeds

For the salad
- 1 fennel bulb, thinly sliced
- 1 red onion, peeled, halved and thinly sliced
- 1 tbsp capers
- 1 tbsp extra virgin olive oil
- Juice of 1 lemon
- Sea salt and freshly ground black pepper, to taste

Serves 6–8 as a sharing plate

Curing fish at home is easy, delicious and fast. It's great to have around to be used when wanted. The ouzo and aniseed flavour here is gentle and delicate and goes really well with the fennel and red onion.

Make sure the fish is super fresh. Mix the salt and sugar together in a bowl. Select a tray or dish that fits the fish neatly. Put half of the sugar-salt mix on the bottom of the dish and place the fillet of fish over the top. Pour over the ouzo and beetroot juice and scatter the fennel seeds over the fillet, then cover it with the rest of the sugar-salt mix. You want the fish to be totally covered so, if necessary, mix some more sugar and salt to cover it completely. Cover with clingfilm or baking parchment and put in the fridge for 24 hours.

Check the firmness of the fish by poking it with your finger – it should feel quite firm. Remove it from the tray and wash it quickly under cold water. Wrap in a clean cloth and let it dry out completely in the fridge.

Make the salad by mixing all the ingredients together in a bowl and seasoning. Cut the fish into thick slices on an angle while leaving the skin behind.

Serve with toasted bread.

Pan-fried Red Mullet with Rosemary, Tomato and Sweet Vinegar

Serves 4

This rosemary and vinegar sauce is an all-round winner and very versatile. I love it with fish but in Crete you often have it with land snails when the season is right. It's definitely one my favourites.

— 4 medium red mullets (about 800g/1lb 12oz), scaled and gutted
— 200ml (7fl oz) extra virgin olive oil, for frying
— Plain flour, for dusting the fish
— 4 sprigs of fresh rosemary
— 2 tbsp chopped tomatoes
— 100ml (3½fl oz) aged white wine vinegar, such as moscatel
— Sea salt, to taste

Wash the fish thoroughly under cold water and keep them in the fridge if you are not going to use them immediately.

Heat a wide frying pan over a medium heat. When it's hot, add enough olive oil to cover the sides of the pan by about 1cm (½in).

Generously salt and dust the cleaned red mullets in the flour and carefully place in the pan. Add the sprigs of rosemary. Cook until golden brown and crispy on one side, turn and do the same for the other. When you turn your fish to cook the other side, add the tomatoes to the pan. This should take about 4 minutes in total. Just before you remove the mullets from the pan, add the vinegar and turn off the heat.

Place the fish on a plate and serve with some of the juices in the pan. You just need a slice of very fresh bread for this and a cold beer.

AEGEAN

Marinated Anchovies with Orange and Lemon, Grilled Peppers and Vine Leaves

Serves 6–8 as a sharing plate

The vine leaves in this recipe play a silent role. They are not usually eaten (even though they could be), but add an amazing aroma to the whole dish that brings the flavours together beautifully.

Place the anchovy fillets in a flat dish and add the orange and lemon juice, vinegar, salt and sugar. Let them sit for about 1 hour. It may take a bit less time depending on the size of the anchovies. They are ready when they have become lighter in colour and stiffer in texture.

Grill or oven roast the peppers at 200°C/400°F/gas mark 6 until they are soft and ready. Place them in a plastic bag or in a bowl covered with clingfilm for 10 minutes and then peel them. Pull them into strips with your hands and discard the seeds and stems.

Line a plate with the vine leaves followed by the peppers. Remove the anchovies from their curing marinade and place them on top. Drizzle some olive oil and scatter the chopped parsley over the top. You may want to add a bit more salt, vinegar or lemon to this but see how you go. Finish the dish with a bit of lemon and orange zest.

- 500g (1lb 2oz) fresh anchovies, gutted and filleted
- Juice of 2 oranges, plus some zest
- Juice of 2 lemons, plus some zest
- 1 tbsp good-quality red wine vinegar
- 2 tsp sea salt
- 1 tsp sugar
- 3 red horn peppers
- 6 preserved vine leaves (make sure they are young and tender)
- 3 tbsp extra virgin olive oil
- 1 tbsp chopped parsley

the SEA

Bitter Leaf Salad with Grape Molasses, Grapes and Crispy Fish Skin

- 300g (10½oz) fish skin from salmon, cod, haddock, hake or another white fish (ask your fishmonger to keep some for you)
- 200ml (7fl oz) vegetable oil, for frying
- 100g (3½oz) plain flour
- 1 small red radicchio
- 1 white chicory
- 1 red chicory
- ½ castelfranco radicchio
- 1 large handful of sultana grapes, cut in half
- 50ml (2fl oz) grape molasses
- 50ml (2fl oz) good-quality red wine vinegar
- 50ml (2fl oz) extra virgin olive oil
- Sea salt, to taste

Serves 4–6 as a sharing plate

I love making this salad when I cure trout or salmon in ouzo. The cured skin is really savoury and delicious. However, you don't need cured fish skin to make this; it's just an idea.

Cut the fish skin into thin strips. Heat the oil in a pan until hot, but not smoking. You can try the oil by adding a tiny piece of the fish skin and seeing whether it starts bubbling instantly.

Dust the strips of fish skin in flour and fry in the hot oil until crispy and golden. Remove from the oil and allow to drain on kitchen paper.

Tear all the leaves by hand and put in a bowl with the grapes. In a small jam jar, add the grape molasses, vinegar, oil and sea salt to taste. Shake vigorously and pour over the leaves. Mix in the crispy fish skin and serve.

Lettuce, Tomato and Bottarga Salad with Fried Crispbread

Serves 4–6 as a sharing plate

I have tried many bottargas in my life – some I love and some I don't. The Trikalinos family in Greece have been producing grey mullet bottarga since 1856. The business was started by three brothers who were just doing what they knew best and theirs is my favourite. Covered in natural beeswax, it is moist and delicate but with a powerful finish. I love to eat it the same way as sea urchins – on toast with a splash of lemon juice and good extra virgin olive oil. The salad here is so simple and aims for the bottarga to be its protagonist.

- 100ml (3½fl oz) vegetable oil, for frying
- 50g (1¾oz) grey mullet bottarga (avgotaraho), cut into slices

For the crispbreads
- 200g (7oz) plain flour
- 2 tsp extra virgin olive oil
- 100ml (3½fl oz) tepid water
- Sea salt, to taste

For the salad
- 1 baby gem lettuce, compact and firm, torn into pieces
- 2 large tomatoes, very ripe and fragrant, sliced into nice thick slices
- 1 small handful of parsley
- 2 tbsp extra virgin olive oil
- Juice of 1 lemon
- Sea salt and freshly ground black pepper, to taste

Make the dough for the crispbreads by adding the flour to a bowl, together with the olive oil and salt. Add the water slowly as you may not need all of it to combine the mixture to a smooth dough. Work the dough on a flat surface for a few minutes and put to one side. It should be silky and elastic. Roll out the dough quite thinly on a floured surface. Make sure you can lift it up easily without tearing. Cut the dough into wonky triangles, depending on the size you prefer.

Heat the vegetable oil until hot but not smoking. Fry the triangles in batches in the oil until golden on both sides. Remove and allow to drain on kitchen paper.

Lay the crispbreads on a plate and layer the baby gem on top. Add the tomato slices and then lay the slices of bottarga over the top. Finish with the whole parsley leaves, drizzle over the oil and lemon juice, and season with salt and pepper.

the SEA

Cured Cod Pastourma with Paprika and Wilted Herb Salad

For the marinade
— 2 tsp smoked hot paprika
— 2 tsp fenugreek
— 1 tsp ground allspice
— 2 tsp ground black pepper
— 2 tsp ground cumin
— 2 tsp sea salt
— 2 tsp sugar
— 1 small handful of sun-dried tomatoes
— 2 garlic cloves, peeled
— 50ml (2fl oz) water

— 200g (7oz) fine sea salt
— 200g (7oz) caster sugar
— 1 cod fillet (approximately 400g/14oz), scaled and boned
— 1 bunch of parsley
— 1 bunch of dill
— 200g (7oz) spinach
— 1 tbsp extra virgin olive oil, plus a little extra
— 1 tsp sea salt
— 1 lemon, quartered

Serves 6–8 as a sharing plate

I remember going to Istanbul and staying on the quieter, greener, Anatolian side. We were having mezze and fish on the side of the Bosphorus and this dish arrived. I had never tried anything like it and loved it. I had only ever eaten beef pastourma in the past, where the meat is cured by salting followed by drying while smothered in 'tsimeni'; a wet paste made predominantly with fenugreek, red peppers and garlic. The cod pastourma recipe was a secret, of course. I was determined to recreate it and tried for months until I was happy with the results. This is a recipe not found in Greece, and certainly not in Crete, but I am confident that it would go down a treat at any traditional village café with old men sipping on raki and bantering about the past.

Put all the marinade ingredients in a food processor and blitz to a smooth paste.

Mix the salt and the sugar in a bowl. Find a container that fits the cod neatly and put half of the sugar-salt mix on the bottom. Rub the cod with the spice paste all over, but go more heavily on the flesh side. Place the fillet on top of the sugar-salt mix and then cover the top of the fish with the remaining mix. You want the fish to be totally covered, so if necessary, mix some more sugar and salt to cover it completely.

Cover with baking parchment, place a lid on the container and place in the fridge for 24 hours. At this point, the fish should be firm. Wash it briefly under cold water (you are only removing the sugar/salt mix not the marinade) and wrap in a clean cloth. Keep it in the fridge until needed.

Roughly chop the parsley, dill and spinach and put in a bowl with the oil and salt. Give them a good rub for a few minutes. Heat a frying pan over a high heat and toss the rubbed herbs for a few minutes. They should not colour but they will wilt and smell divine.

Slice the cod on an angle into thin slices, leaving behind the skin. Cover the base of a plate with the wilted herbs and place the cod slices over the top. Finish with a drizzle of olive oil and lemon wedges.

the SEA

Rice with Limpets and Cretan Wine

Serves 4

- 500g (1lb 2oz) fresh limpets
- 2 tbsp extra virgin olive oil
- 1 white onion, finely diced
- 400g (14oz) tomatoes, blitzed in a food processor
- 1 tbsp butter
- 1 tsp dried oregano
- 1 tsp thyme, chopped
- 150g (5½oz) short-grain rice
- 200ml (7fl oz) Cretan marouvas wine or Spanish dry sherry, like fino or manzanilla, or orange wine
- Juice of 1–2 lemons

I tried this recipe 10 years ago, at Babis's house in Falasarna, 40 minutes drive west of Chania. Babis was my dad's best friend, a great fisherman and a very funny man. He knew me before I remember knowing him. Food played a big role in his household and both his mother and wife were impeccable cooks. Whenever I unexpectedly returned to Crete for a few days, Babis was the first to find out and always made me feel special with a great feast. It usually involved him killing a hen or cockerel and cooking rice, but this one time his wife had foraged some limpets and made this.

Every household in Crete has a bottle or a barrel of Cretan wine, known as marouvas. It is usually made from Romeiko grapes and aged for a good amount of time. It is high in alcohol and its natural oxidation gives it complexity and unique aromas. I find that marouvas has a lot in common with the Spanish fino and manzanilla dry sherries. Even though these sherries are fortified to reach their high alcohol volume, their flavour has been affected by natural yeasts that develop in the barrels.

Orange wines, made by allowing the skin of white wine grapes to stay in contact with the juice during fermentation, can also be used when the above aren't available. When the grape skin has remained in contact for over 5 months, these wines have a delicate yet complex structure – they are light and elegant, like a white wine, but have an intensity and bitterness resembling a red.

The limpets should still be alive when you buy them. Wash them well under cold water. Bring a pot of water to the boil and drop in the limpets for a few minutes. Remove from the pot using a slotted spoon and, when cool enough to handle, use a teaspoon to remove the flesh from the shells. Put to one side. Pass the cooking water through a sieve and preserve.

Heat the olive oil in a pan and cook the onion until translucent and sweet. Add the tomatoes, butter, oregano and thyme and cook for 10 minutes over a medium heat. Add the rice, wine and limpets to the pot and stir occasionally. If the rice is drying up, add some of the limpet cooking water – you want the rice to be juicy and fall off a spoon easily, so make sure it doesn't dry up.

The rice should take about 20 minutes to cook. When ready, turn the heat off and add the lemon juice. Stir and serve immediately. I like serving this with some lemony aioli (see page 71).

AEGEAN

Cuttlefish Stew with Bitter Green Olives, Artichokes and Red Ripe Tomatoes

Serves 6–8 as a sharing plate

This stew is typcially served in Crete in homes rather than restaurants. What I love most about this dish is that all the attention is given to the olives. Once they are harvested in the winter months, they are cured and stored in large jars, brought out with pride when the batch is ready, so the cuttlefish stew can be made.

— 3 large artichokes, prepared and hearts sliced thinly
— 100ml (3½fl oz) olive oil
— 1kg (2lb 4oz) whole cuttlefish, cleaned and cut into bite-sized pieces
— 3 garlic cloves, peeled and crushed
— 3 thyme sprigs, stalks discarded
— 4 bay leaves
— 300ml (½ pint) good-quality white wine
— 400g (14oz) ripe red tomatoes, blitzed in a food processor
— 100g (3½oz) bitter green olives, with stones in
— Sea salt, to taste

The artichokes I'm used to in Crete can be very spiky and need to be handled with a lot of care. The ones in the UK are usually easier to prepare. If the artichoke has a stem, cut it off as it's quite tough. Using your fingers, start pulling away the green leaves and discard them. If they are too tough, use a pair of scissors. Stop removing the leaves as soon as you reach the pale tender ones. Cut the artichoke in half lengthways, pull away the purple leaves at the centre and the hairy 'choke', which is inedible. Trim away any tough dark green bits. Slice the artichokes and place them in a bowl with water and half a lemon (to stop them discolouring).

Heat a pan over a medium heat and, when hot, add the oil and cuttlefish. Increase the heat and cook for a few minutes. Add the garlic, thyme, bay leaves and wine to the pan and continue to cook over a high heat for a few more minutes. Add the tomatoes to the pan and turn down the heat to low. Cover with a lid and allow to cook gently for 20 minutes. Add the sliced artichokes and olives and check the seasoning. Sometimes if the olives are quite salty, you may not want to add any more salt. Cook gently for another 20 minutes or until the cuttlefish is really tender, the artichokes are soft and the sauce has thickened.

I like to serve this dish with fried chips in olive oil or with a baked potato with capers and anchovies (see page 76).

the SEA

Smoked and Fresh Fish Fishcakes with Capers and Lemony Aioli

Makes about 15 fishcakes

This is another dish we made at the restaurant in Crete, created because we had all this miscellaneous fish my dad caught that we couldn't sell. We used lots of cod-like fish, eels, flat fish and whatever else came our way really. We would boil the fish in water and then the mission of removing spikes and skin began. Imagine a massive pile of fish in front of you that you would have to go through to end up with beautiful boneless white flesh. It took hours and a lot of patience, but the end result was completely worth it.

— 800g (1lb 12oz) Cyprus potatoes, peeled and chopped
— 400g (14oz) smoked haddock fillet
— 300g (10½oz) fresh cod fillet
— 150ml (¼ pint) milk
— 200ml (7fl oz) water
— 1 garlic clove, peeled
— 2 tsp lemon thyme, chopped
— 2 tbsp fresh parsley, chopped
— 3–4 fresh basil leaves, chopped
— ⅓ Scotch bonnet chilli, deseeded and chopped finely
— 2 tbsp capers
— 2 organic eggs
— 200g (7oz) breadcrumbs
— 500ml (18fl oz) vegetable oil
— Sea salt and freshly ground black pepper, to taste

For the lemony aioli
— 4 tbsp mayonnaise
— Juice of 2 lemons
— 1 tsp Dijon mustard
— 1 tsp white wine vinegar
— 2 garlic cloves, crushed with a touch of oil into a paste

Put the potatoes in a saucepan with water and boil until soft. Remove from the pan with a slotted spoon and place in a colander to dry out.

Place the fish fillets (cut them to fit if needed) in another pan and add the milk, water and garlic. Gently simmer for about 5 minutes. Remove the fish from the liquid and put to one side to cool down.

Mash the potatoes in a bowl using your hands or a potato masher and add the lemon thyme, parsley, basil, chilli and capers to the bowl. Using your fingertips, mash the fish up, removing any skin and bones you come across, and add to the bowl with the potatoes. Mix everything together really well and adjust the seasoning.

Quickly make the lemony aioli by mixing all the ingredients in a bowl. Place in the fridge until needed.

Mould the fishcakes using your hands into plum-sized balls and then gently flatten them. Beat the eggs in a bowl and spread out the breadcrumbs on a large plate.

Heat the vegetable oil in a medium frying pan. Dip the fishcakes, one by one, first into the egg and then into the breadcrumbs. Make sure they are well coated and don't pat them to remove extra crumbs. When the oil is hot but not smoky, fry the fishcakes until golden and crispy on one side and then flip to do the same on the other. Remove from the pan and place on kitchen paper to drain the excess oil. Serve with a nice dollop of aioli on the side and some fresh bread.

the SEA

AEGEAN

Shaved Cuttlefish with Tomato Butter Sauce and Parsley

Serves 4–6 as a sharing plate

Cleaning cuttlefish can be a messy business, so ask your fishmonger to do it and it will save you lots of time cleaning an ink-covered sink. By 'shaving' the cuttlefish so thinly, you create a texture that is really satisfying and it also reduces the cooking time significantly.

- 600g (1lb 5oz) fresh cuttlefish, cleaned
- 1 tbsp extra virgin olive oil
- 100g (3½oz) good-quality butter
- 1 garlic clove, chopped
- 400g (14oz) ripe red tomatoes, blitzed in a food processor
- 3 fresh bay leaves
- 3–4 fresh basil leaves (I use Greek basil leaves – they are tiny and very aromatic)
- Sea salt and freshly ground black pepper, to taste

Using a very sharp knife, slice the cuttlefish as thinly as possible. You want it to be paper-thin ideally.

Heat a frying pan over a medium heat and, when hot, add the olive oil quickly followed by the cuttlefish. It will be hot and smoky, so be careful that oil doesn't splash on you. When the cuttlefish is beginning to get some colour and is shrivelling a bit, remove from the pan and place in a bowl together with any juices. This process should take about 5 minutes.

Place the pan back on the heat and add the butter. When the butter starts to turn golden, add the garlic and cook for a minute or two. Add the tomatoes, bay and basil leaves and season the sauce with salt and pepper. Allow to cook for 5 minutes and add the cuttlefish back into the pan. Cook gently for 10–15 minutes or until the cuttlefish is soft and buttery.

I like eating this with a simple rocket salad with lots of lemon juice and extra virgin olive oil.

Oven-baked Potatoes with Capers and Anchovies

Serves 4–6 as a sharing plate

This dish is simple and so delicious. It's perfect on its own with a leafy salad, and a great accompaniment to lamb or fish. If you fancy making it even richer, you can always add a dash of double cream.

Preheat the oven to 180°C/350°F/gas mark 4.

Slice the potatoes on a mandolin very thinly and place in a colander with a touch of salt for 15 minutes.

Fry the peppers in 1 tablespoon of olive oil for a few minutes until soft.

Blitz the tomatoes, peppers, capers and anchovy fillets to a paste. Transfer the drained potatoes to an oven dish and add the wine, remaining oil, oregano, black pepper and anchovy paste to the dish. Mix everything really well with your hands and check the seasoning. Flatten the potatoes and cover with baking parchment. Bake in the oven for about 40 minutes and then check whether the potatoes are nice and soft. When this is the case, remove the parchment and put back into the oven until a nice golden crust has formed on the top layer.

Remove from the oven and serve with the cuttlefish stew (see page 70). The combination is intense as the flavours are strong in both dishes but they are perfect and as savoury as it gets.

- 4 medium waxy potatoes
- 2 green peppers, deseeded and sliced
- 4 tbsp extra virgin olive oil
- 200g (7oz) red tomatoes
- 2 tbsp capers
- 8 anchovy fillets
- 200ml (7fl oz) white wine
- 2 tsp dried oregano
- 1 tsp freshly black ground pepper
- Sea salt, to taste

the SEA

AEGEAN

Fried Squid, Samphire and Cold Beer

Serves 4

There is nothing to this dish in terms of complexity or skill, but knowing how to fry a squid nicely makes all the difference. Firstly the squid needs to be super fresh. If it is large, it may need tenderizing; after you have cut it, put it in a colander with 1 teaspoon of salt and massage it firmly for 3–4 minutes. The tentacles in its head will spring up when sufficiently tender. Before you cook the squid, you need to make sure you have seasoned it perfectly. Adding salt after it has been fried will never stick and it won't be the same. You need to make sure that the squid is slightly wet before you toss it in the flour so you get a nice crispy layer. Also, ensuring the oil is hot enough makes all the difference in creating the best fried squid.

The samphire is crunchy and salty and goes beautifully with the squid and, of course, don't forget a cold beer.

- 200g (7oz) plain flour
- 70g (2½oz) semolina
- 500g (1lb 2oz) really fresh squid, cleaned and cut into thick rings
- 200–300ml (7–10fl oz) vegetable oil, for frying
- 200g (7oz) samphire
- 1 tbsp extra virgin olive oil
- 3 lemons, 1 juiced, 2 halved for serving
- Sea salt and freshly ground black pepper, to taste

Mix the flour and semolina on a plate and season the squid generously with salt and pepper. Toss in the flour and semolina mix and let it sit in there for a few minutes.

Heat the oil in a tall pot, making sure the oil does not come more than halfway up otherwise it will overflow when the squid goes in, which can be dangerous. When the oil is very hot but not smoky, shake the excess flour off the squid and very carefully lower the squid into the oil.

Resist shaking the squid for the first few minutes as you don't want the flour to fall off. Then shake gently every so often to ensure that all the rings are separate. When the squid is crunchy and golden, remove from the oil using a slotted spoon and place on kitchen paper to drain the excess oil.

Mix the samphire with the olive oil and lemon juice and serve alongside the squid. Eat immediately with lots of lemon for squeezing.

If you fancy, you can also serve this with a bit of lemony aioli (see page 71).

Courgette and Feta Fritters

Serves 4–6 as a sharing plate

In the summer months in our restaurant, we used to grate about 10kg (24lb) of courgettes every evening for these. It was incredible how many of them would be ordered. We used just feta in the original recipe but the addition of some hard cheese only makes them better. They are a perfect snack after a long day on the beach.

— 4 large courgettes
— 1 large red onion, diced
— 1 tbsp olive oil
— 1 large handful of fresh mint leaves, chopped
— 1 handful of fresh dill, chopped
— 100g (3½oz) feta, crumbled
— 100g (3½oz) strong hard cheese, such as Manchego, Pecorino or Parmesan, coarsely grated
— 4 tbsp plain flour (possibly a bit more), plus extra for dusting
— 2 organic eggs
— 1 tsp dried oregano
— 200ml (7fl oz) vegetable oil, for frying
— Sea salt and freshly ground black pepper, to taste

Grate the courgettes using the coarse side of a box grater, then salt them and let them drain for 10 minutes.

Fry the red onion gently in the olive oil until translucent. Squeeze the courgettes to get rid of excess water and place in a bowl with the onion. Add the mint and dill, feta and hard cheese. Add the flour and eggs and mix everything together. Season with oregano, salt and pepper. The mix will be quite loose but manageable enough to create the fritters. Check for seasoning.

Heat the oil until hot but not smoking. Check by dropping in a bit of the mixture – it should bubble instantly. Take a large tablespoon of the mix, roll in the flour and fry in the hot oil until golden. Repeat until all the mix is used up.

Cretan Ntakos (Barley Rusks with Grated Tomato and Goat's Cheese)

Serves 4–6 as a sharing plate

Cretan ntakos is, without doubt, the best quick snack during the summer months. It is traditionally a cold dish made with barley rusks, grated tomatoes and creamy fresh mizithra cheese. It's usually made when the tomatoes are so ripe you can smell them being grated from a distance. For us, it was the snack to have after a long day on the beach, sitting on the veranda with a cold beer and getting ready for the evening stroll.

This version is the one you will typically find in Crete during the summer months. If you are unable to find a nice fresh goat's curd, you can blitz some feta with a touch of olive oil and a splash of water until thick and silky and pour that on top of your tomatoes. If the feta is very acidic, add a teaspoon of sugar when blitzing.

- 3–4 very ripe red tomatoes
- 2–4 Cretan barley rusks (paksimadia), depending on size
- 150g (5½oz) Cretan mizithra (traditional goat's cheese) or fresh goat's curd
- 1 small handful of good-quality olives with stones, preferably black
- Extra virgin olive oil
- 1 tsp oregano
- Sea salt, to taste

Grate the tomatoes using the coarse side of a box grater and place in a bowl.

To serve, place the rusks in a shallow bowl and spoon the grated tomato on top. Arrange the goat's cheese on top of the tomato and scatter over the olives. Pour a generous amount of olive oil over the top and sprinkle with some sea salt and oregano.

Cretan Ntakos
with Aubergine

Serves 4–6 as a sharing plate

This second version (see pages 84–85) is served warm and is richer than the first as here the topping is cooked slowly. Despite the fact that you may not be able to find this in Greece, it is absolutely delicious and a great alternative when the fragrant sun-ripened tomatoes are not available.

If you are unable to find a nice fresh goat's curd, you can blitz some feta with a touch of olive oil and a splash of water until thick and silky and pour that over your topping. If the feta is very acidic, add a teaspoon of sugar when blitzing.

For the topping
— 80ml (2¾fl oz) extra virgin olive oil
— Small bunch of fresh sage leaves, stems removed
— 2 garlic cloves, finely chopped
— 3 red horn peppers (or romano), diced
— 50g (1¾oz) sun-dried tomatoes, chopped
— 1 large aubergine, diced
— 100g (3½oz) blanched almonds
— 100g (3½oz) cherry tomatoes, roughly chopped

— 150g (5½oz) Cretan mizithra or fresh goat's curd
— 2–4 Cretan barley rusks (paksimadia)
— Sea salt and freshly ground black pepper, to taste

For the dressing
— 6 tbsp extra virgin olive oil
— 2 tbsp aged red wine vinegar
— Sea salt, to taste

Heat a frying pan over a medium heat and add the olive oil. Gently place the sage leaves in the oil and fry until crispy. Remove from the pan and place on kitchen paper to absorb any excess oil.

Add the garlic to the pan and brown gently. When golden, add all the remaining topping ingredients, cover and cook gently with a lid until soft, creamy and sweet. This may take about 20–25 minutes. Adjust the seasoning and remove from the heat.

Put the dressing ingredients in a jar and shake well.

Soak the rusks under cold water for one second (to assist softening). Put them on a plate, spoon over the topping and arrange the goat's cheese on top. Finish with the dressing and the crispy sage leaves.

AEGEAN

Cretan Summer Salad with Fresh Cheese and Traditional Rusks

- 3 medium, ripe red tomatoes, cut into bite-sized pieces
- 1 crisp cucumber, peeled, cut in half lengthways and then into thin half-moon pieces
- 1 green pepper, halved and sliced
- 1 small red onion, cut in half and then into thin wedges
- A handful of good-quality olives with stones (we use black wrinkly Greek olives)
- 1 tbsp capers
- 1 tbsp chopped flat-leaf parsley
- 1 handful of purslane, if available, or rocket leaves, chopped
- 1 tsp dried oregano
- 4 small Cretan barley rusks (paksimadia) or 2 large ones, broken into bite-sized pieces
- 60ml (2½fl oz) extra virgin olive oil
- 3 tbsp good-quality aged red wine vinegar
- 150g (5½oz) Cretan mizithra or feta, crumbled
- Sea salt, to taste

Serves 4–6 as a sharing plate

A Cretan salad is in fact very similar to the well-known Greek salad, but has mizithra – traditional goat's cheese – or goat's curd instead of feta as well as broken Cretan barley rusks. Sometimes you may also find capers or caper leaves, purslane and even a few leaves of basil. For me, this is one of the best salads to have with a meal, especially grilled fish, or even just make a big bowl and eat it with nothing more.

Finding Cretan barley rusks may not be the easiest thing unless you live close to a Greek deli. However, there are many alternatives you can use instead that are readily available on the market. Swedish crispbreads are a good alternative and can be easily found, but thickly sliced sourdough drizzled with olive oil and dried out in a preheated oven at 160°C/325°F/ gas mark 3 would be my choice.

Add all the salad ingredients to a bowl, apart from the cheese, and mix gently. Let it sit for a few minutes and then add the cheese. Mix once more and serve.

the LAND

AEGEAN

Stuffed Courgette Flowers with Fresh Cheese and Honey

Makes 12

Fried cheese and honey is a pairing from heaven. Adding courgette flowers to the equation is just irresistible. These amazing edible flowers have a short season so when they arrive it's worth making as much as possible with them. Whether they are stuffed with rice, joining other stuffed vegetables in the oven; stuffed with greens and cheese; or as they are here, they are the best spring/early summer treat and I find myself patiently anticipating their arrival every year.

— 200g (7oz) Cretan mizithra or fresh goat's curd
— 50g (1¾oz) sugar
— 12 courgette flowers
— 100g (3½oz) self-raising flour
— ½ can of lager (approximately)
— 200ml (7fl oz) vegetable oil
— 2–3 tbsp good-quality honey, depending on preference
— Sea salt, to taste

Mix the goat's curd with the sugar. Gently open the petals of each flower and, using a teaspoon, distribute the goat's curd equally. Close the petals to seal the cheese.

Make a batter with the flour and beer and season with salt. The batter should resemble thick double cream so, depending on your flour, you may need more or less beer.

Heat the oil in a frying pan over a medium heat. Check it's hot enough by dropping in a teaspoon of batter – it should bubble instantly. Dip each flower in the batter and lower into the hot oil. Cook for about 6 minutes or until golden brown on both sides. Remove from the pan and place on kitchen paper to remove the excess oil. Pile on a plate, drizzle with the honey and eat straight away.

I love to have these with a pot of Cretan mountain tea, which is very aromatic and herbaceous and complements the stuffed courgette flowers beautifully.

Also, if the mood is right and the place calls for it, a shot or two of tsikoudia (Cretan raki) is a very good accompaniment.

the LAND

Stuffed Courgettes with Lemon Sauce

— 2–3 green and yellow courgettes
(try to get large ones as they
are easier to hollow out)

For the stuffing
— 4 tbsp extra virgin olive oil,
plus a little extra
— 200g (7oz) minced beef
— 2–3 medium tomatoes,
finely chopped
— 6 tbsp round (short-grain) rice
— 2 handfuls of chard or spinach,
finely chopped
— 1 handful of fresh mint leaves,
finely chopped
— 1 handful of fresh parsley,
finely chopped
— 1 handful of fresh dill,
finely chopped
— 2 tbsp lemon juice
— 1 tsp each of oregano, cinnamon,
allspice
— 3 tbsp pine nuts
— 2 tbsp raisins
— Sea salt and freshly ground
black pepper, to taste

For the sauce
— 2 organic egg yolks
— Juice of 2 lemons
— 1 tsp plain flour, sifted

Serves 4–6 as a sharing plate

I remember having to hollow dozens of courgettes for this dish as a kid. They always said that kids were best for this job as our hands were small and delicate so we wouldn't break the courgettes. Nowadays, I halve them and then hollow them, so the cylinder is short and easier to hollow out. This dish can be found all over Greece with small variations, depending on locality and, of course, household. I like to add tomatoes, spinach and lots of herbs to keep the dish fresh and light. The lemon and egg sauce is a classic and makes the courgettes creamy and moreish.

Cut the courgettes into 5cm (2in) cylinders. Using a teaspoon, gently and carefully remove the flesh from the inside, creating a hollow tube closed on one end. If by mistake you open both sides of the courgette, don't worry too much. You can use another vegetable or a thin slice of the courgette to seal the hole. Sprinkle some salt on the courgettes and put to one side.

Heat a pan over a medium heat and add 2 tablespoons of the olive oil. Brown the minced beef, season with salt and pepper, remove from the heat and put in a bowl.

In a separate bowl, add half of the tomatoes, together with all the other stuffing ingredients, including the beef, and mix well. Stuff the courgettes with this mix and place them neatly into a pan. Pour the remaining tomato and the remaining olive oil over the courgettes with enough water to cover the courgettes halfway. Cover with a lid and cook gently for 30–40 minutes or until the courgettes are soft and the rice is cooked.

In a separate bowl, whisk together the yolks, lemon juice and flour and pour over the courgettes. Turn the heat to the lowest setting and shake the pan gently until the sauce begins to thicken.

Serve the courgettes hot or cold with some extra fresh herbs.

Stuffed Courgette Flowers with Goat's Curd and Anchovies

Makes 12

This is another way to enjoy these beautiful flowers. The really savoury anchovies and sun-dried tomatoes make a great combination with the creamy goat's curd. This dish is amazing as part of a mezze, with a glass of cold beer or a shot of raki.

Preheat the oven to 180°C/350°F/gas mark 4.

Place all the ingredients for the stuffing in a bowl and mix well. Carefully open the petals of the flower and, using a teaspoon, distribute the mixture evenly. Then close the petals again to seal the stuffing.

Place on a small lined baking tray – ideally one that just fits them – and drizzle with olive oil and a splash of water. Cover with baking parchment and place in the oven for 20–25 minutes. Remove the parchment and cook for a few minutes longer until golden on the surface.

— 12 courgette flowers
— Extra virgin olive oil, for drizzling

For the stuffing
— 200g (7oz) Cretan mizithra or fresh goat's curd (feta also works fine)
— 100g (3½oz) courgette, grated
— 6 cured anchovy fillets, chopped
— 50g (1¾oz) sun-dried tomatoes, finely chopped
— 1 handful of fresh mint leaves, chopped

the LAND

AEGEAN

Cretan Courgette and Feta Bake with Sesame

- 4 medium Cyprus potatoes, peeled (about 800g/1lb 12oz)
- 4 medium pale green courgettes (about 800g/1lb 12oz)
- 1 tsp sea salt
- 1 large bunch of mint leaves, chopped
- 240g (8½oz) good-quality feta, crumbled
- 100g (3½oz) mature sheep's milk cheese, such as Cretan Graviera or Spanish Manchego, grated
- 200g (7oz) ripe red tomatoes, roughly chopped
- 80ml (2¾fl oz) extra virgin olive oil
- 1 tsp dried oregano
- 1 tbsp sesame seeds
- 1 tsp black sesame seeds
- Sea salt and freshly ground black pepper, to taste

Serves 4–6 as a sharing plate

This bake is often found encased in olive oil pastry; however, this method makes it lighter and also a great accompaniment to poultry.

Slice the potatoes and courgettes thinly using a mandolin. If you don't have one, use a knife and go as thin as possible. Sprinkle with the teaspoon of salt and let them sit for 10–15 minutes.

Preheat the oven to 180°C/350°F/gas mark 4. Put all the remaining ingredients, except for both types of sesame seeds, into a bowl and mix well with your hands. Add the potatoes and courgettes and give everything another good mix. You want both the potatoes and courgettes coated beautifully with the cheese mix. Adjust the seasoning if needed and transfer them to a baking tray, pressing down the mix a bit to make it slightly compact. Scatter the white and black sesame seeds over the top.

Place a sheet of kitchen foil or baking parchment on top and bake in the oven for about 30–40 minutes or until the potatoes are soft. Remove the foil or parchment and cook for another 10 minutes so the top of the bake becomes lovely and golden.

Remove from the oven and enjoy hot or cold. Most people say that this bake is much tastier the next day when all the ingredients have had time to give out their best flavours.

Watermelon, Charred Feta and Bread Salad with Mint

Serves 4–6 as a sharing plate

I was introduced to feta and watermelon more than 20 years ago when a very good friend of mine, Nina Salpigidou, used to eat the two together with a slice of fresh bread. I still remember thinking that she was absolutely mad. I could not possibly contemplate how on earth those three ingredients could be eaten together. Who would have imagined that many years after that initial exposure, I would come to think that a fresh watermelon and feta salad is actually the best summer snack ever?

Sometimes I feel this salad needs a touch of sweet vinegar and at other times I feel it's perfect with the oil, salt and pepper. I think all this depends on the acidity of the feta and the sweetness of the watermelon. If you think you need it to be sharper, then add a splash of good-quality vinegar.

- 2 slices of sourdough bread, cut into small squares
- 7 tbsp extra virgin olive oil
- 500g (1lb 2oz) watermelon flesh, cut into small bite-sized pieces, pips removed
- 10 black Greek olives, pitted
- 1 handful of fresh mint, chopped
- 1 tbsp pumpkin seeds
- 1 small cucumber, sliced lengthways and then across into thin half-moon pieces
- 1 handful of purslane, if available, or rocket leaves, roughly chopped
- 200g (7oz) feta, cut into medium-sized cubes
- Sea salt and freshly ground black pepper, to taste

Preheat the oven to 160°C/325°F/gas mark 3.

Spread the sourdough croutons on a baking tray, drizzle with 2 tablespoons of olive oil and bake in the oven until golden – this should take around 10 minutes.

Put all the remaining ingredients, apart from the feta, in a bowl and mix gently. Season to taste.

Just before you serve the salad, put the feta on a lined baking tray and place under a hot grill for a minute or two, until it slightly colours at the edges. Add the hot feta and toasted sourdough to the bowl and give the salad a final mix before serving.

AEGEAN

Chilled Watermelon and Cucumber Soup

Makes 8–10 small glasses

Summer in Crete means a huge daily consumption of watermelons, usually just cut into massive chunks and eaten really cold. As children we often entered the not-so-well-behaved pip-spitting competition, in which we had to hit various targets from a distance, sometimes human ones. As we grew up, we used to tie watermelons with ropes and cool them in the sea water while camping, then inject some vodka into them and force straws through the flesh. A very fresh cocktail I must say.

The farmers sell their produce from the back of their vans in countless spots around the island. The scene is amazing. An overloaded trunk, a pair of scales and a piece of cardboard with the price per kilo written in bad handwriting. The watermelons are enormous and they weigh much the same as a small child.

— Approximately 1kg (2lb 4oz) watermelon flesh, rind and pips removed
— 3 cucumbers, grated and sprinkled with 1 tsp sea salt
— 80g (2¾oz) sourdough bread
— 3 tbsp aged red wine vinegar
— 50ml (1¾oz) extra virgin olive oil (not too strong)
— 1 tbsp Turkish chilli flakes
— Sea salt and freshly ground pepper, to taste
— Some fresh mint leaves, to serve
— Fried bread and feta crunch, to garnish (optional)

For the fried bread and feta crunch
— 2 tbsp extra virgin olive oil
— 2 medium slices of sourdough, cubed
— 100g (3½oz) feta, crumbled

Place a sieve over a bowl and squeeze the watermelon into it with your hands, crushing it as much as possible to collect the juice. You should have 500ml (18fl oz) of juice. Do the same with the cucumbers and you should end up with 150ml (¼ pint) of cucumber juice.

Place both juices in a food processor and add the bread, vinegar, olive oil and chilli flakes. Blitz until everything becomes smooth and silky. Season with salt and pepper to taste and chill for at least 30 minutes.

Serve in glasses with ice and fresh mint leaves.

I like to sprinkle the fried bread and feta crunch over the soup just before serving, as it makes it super-delicious and adds texture. However, it is also very good without it as a chilled vegan soup that's perfect on a hot summer's day.

Heat the oil in a frying pan over a medium heat and add the bread. Cook gently until golden and crispy all round. Remove from the pan and place on kitchen paper to absorb the excess oil. Roughly blitz the bread in a food processor and return to the pan with the crumbled feta. Cook gently until the mix dries out. Remove and place on kitchen paper to soak up some of the oil. Set aside until needed.

AEGEAN

Green Leaf Salad with Figs, Pomegranate and Sesame Brittle

Serves 4–6 as a sharing salad

With the bitter leaves, tangy pomegranate, sweet figs and sesame snaps, this delicious salad covers all the requirements for a good salad. I love having it with grilled fish or even some feta baked in foil.

Clean and prepare the salad leaves carefully and toss gently in a bowl so they are evenly mixed. Sprinkle over the chopped mint, pomegranate seeds, sliced figs and sesame snap pieces and dress with the olive oil, vinegar, honey, salt and pepper. Serve immediately.

- 1 baby gem lettuce, cut into thin wedges
- 1 white chicory, leaves separated
- 1 head of radicchio or other red leaves, roughly sliced
- 1 head of fennel, cut in quarters, then sliced very thinly
- 1 handful of fresh mint leaves, roughly chopped
- 4 tbsp pomegranate seeds
- 8 fresh figs, sliced thinly
- 60g (2½oz) sesame snaps, broken into small pieces
- 6 tbsp extra virgin olive oil
- 2–3 tbsp aged sweet red wine vinegar
- 1 tbsp good-quality honey
- Sea salt and freshly ground pepper, to taste

the LAND

Cheese and Yogurt Dip with Chillies and Marjoram

Serves 4–6 as a sharing plate

This is a version of the Greek 'tirokafteri', which basically means spicy cheese. As with lots of classics, every household has its own version and this is mine. If you prefer yours to be spicier, then simply add more chillies, but remember that their heat develops as the dip rests.

- 1 red horn pepper, deseeded
- 2 red chillies, deseeded
- 1 green chilli, deseeded
- 200g (7oz) feta
- 1 tbsp chopped parsley, plus extra to garnish
- 40ml (1½fl oz) extra virgin olive oil
- 1 tbsp Greek yogurt
- 2 tsp dried marjoram
- 1 tsp dried oregano
- 1 tsp ground black pepper
- Sea salt, to taste

Char the pepper and chillies in a dry hot pan until they begin to darken a little on the outside. You can also do this under the grill or on a griddle.

Remove from the pan and peel off as much as the skin as you can. Don't worry if it won't come off completely.

Add all the ingredients to a food processor and blitz until smooth. Adjust the seasoning and serve with some extra parsley, fresh bread, olives and raw vegetables. Some people love to add a bit of lemon juice over the top but this is up to you – the acidity is good without it. I also love to have this dip with grilled lamb cutlets or grilled meat in general.

Chilled Yogurt, Apricot and Pine Nut Dip

Serves 4–6 as a sharing plate

This is a great dish to have on the table when eating grilled meats. It's cool and refreshing and the apricots add a sweet twist to it.

- 1 cucumber, grated using the coarse side of a box grater
- 100g (3½oz) dried apricots
- 1 handful of mint leaves
- 400g (14oz) strained Greek yogurt
- 1 tbsp pine nuts, dry toasted
- 1 garlic clove, crushed
- 100ml (3½fl oz) extra virgin olive oil
- 1 tsp white wine vinegar
- Sea salt, to taste

Coarsely grate the whole cucumber. Finely chop the apricots and mint. Place all the ingredients in a bowl and mix well. Adjust the seasoning and chill in the fridge until needed. Make sure you have some nice bread to eat with this.

the LAND

AEGEAN

Dried Broad
Bean Dip

Serves 6–8 as a sharing plate

Broad beans, known as 'koukia' in Greek, are not to be confused with what Greeks refer to as fava beans, as the latter are yellow split peas and are used to make the popular Greek fava purée. Fresh broad beans are a favourite during spring and are very often eaten raw with some sea salt and a shot of 'tsikoudia' (raki), or cooked with lamb and artichokes. For the rest of the year, the dried beans are turned into soups and stews, as well as delicious dips and spreads like the one below. This is perfect with fresh bread or spread on toast with some freshly sliced tomatoes and a few olives.

- 200g (7oz) dried broad beans, soaked overnight in water
- 2 garlic cloves
- 250g (9oz) red ripe tomatoes
- 1 red onion, peeled and quartered
- 100ml (3½fl oz) good-quality red wine
- 50ml (2fl oz) extra virgin olive oil
- 3 bay leaves
- ½ tsp chilli powder
- ½ tsp ground nutmeg
- 1 small cinnamon stick
- 2 cloves, crushed
- 8 juniper berries, crushed
- Sea salt, to taste

After you have soaked the beans overnight, give them a very good wash under cold running water and tip them into a large pan. Make sure you add a generous amount of water to the pan so that the beans are covered by about 5cm (2in).

Cook the beans for about 1 hour – you may need to top up the water during this time. The beans should be soft at this point and the water just covering them. Add all the remaining ingredients to the pan, stir well and cover with a lid. Lower the heat and continue cooking for another 40 minutes or so.

The beans should have broken down now and the mix should be shiny and thick. Adjust the seasoning, take out the cinnamon and bay leaves and remove from the heat. You can eat this hot or cold; it's delicious both ways.

the LAND

AEGEAN

Tomato and Oregano Fritters with Whipped Feta

Makes about 12 fritters

During the summer months, when schools were shut, I would wake up in the morning and go downstairs to Theía Koula's house. Theía means 'Auntie', but the truth is that she is not my real auntie. She is much more than that. She and her husband, Theíos Nikos, planted the seeds of the love for food that I have today. With utter patience and goodwill, they taught me, looked after me and gifted me with memories that will always stay with me. Theía Koula and I would sit in the kitchen at her large wooden table, covered with a plastic tablecloth with fake lace, and sip on Greek coffee with sweet sesame biscuits. She cooked the purest food I have ever known. She had animals, a garden, olive trees, grape vines and she knew everything there was to know about wild food in Crete. Everything on her kitchen table was grown by her or made by her hands. I realize now what a luxury that was.

When the sun was hot and the tomatoes tasted like honey, we would make the best tomato fritters. I still remember the first time I tasted them. You can smell the tomatoes before you see them; the fresh mint, the wild oregano – the whole kitchen bursting with sweetness and summer aromas. I would often go tomato picking with Theía Koula in her garden. She was very particular about her tomatoes; one basket would be for the ones she used for cooking and the other for the ones she used for eating – meaning the ones she ate raw in salads.

- 400g (14oz) really ripe tomatoes, finely diced
- 1 red onion, finely diced
- 1 tbsp oregano leaves, preferably wild
- 4 tbsp fresh mint leaves, chopped
- 6 tbsp self-raising flour (you may need a bit more)
- 500ml (18fl oz) vegetable oil, for frying
- Sea salt and freshly ground black pepper, to taste

For the whipped feta
- 100g (3½oz) good-quality feta
- 1 tsp extra virgin olive oil
- 1 tbsp water
- ½ tsp sugar

Make the whipped feta by blitzing all the ingredients together until smooth and silky. Transfer to a bowl and put in the fridge.

Put all the fritter ingredients in a bowl except the oil. Season generously with salt and pepper and mix well. The mixture should be neither too stiff nor too runny. You want to be able to lift a spoonful of it and drop it into the oil. If it's too runny, add more flour, but don't overdo it as they will be bready.

Heat the oil for frying the fritters in a saucepan over a medium heat. Make sure the oil comes at least 2cm (¾in) up the sides of the pan. Check the oil is hot enough by dropping in a tiny bit of the mix – it should bubble instantly. Lower spoonfuls of the mix into the hot oil. Turn down the heat and cook the fritters on both sides until golden, about 5–6 minutes. Remove from the oil and place on kitchen paper to absorb any excess oil. Eat immediately with the whipped feta on the side.

the LAND

Chilled Cucumber Soup with Fried Courgettes and Spiced Almonds

For the soup
- 4 cucumbers (about 700g/1lb 9oz), roughly chopped
- 2 garlic cloves, chopped
- 1 small bunch of dill, chopped
- 150g (5½oz) thick Greek yogurt
- 100ml (3½fl oz) water
- 1 tsp good-quality vinegar
- Sea salt and freshly ground black pepper, to taste

For the spiced almonds
- 100g (3½oz) raw unsalted almonds, with skins on
- 1 tbsp butter
- 1 tbsp black sesame seeds
- 1 tsp black onion seeds
- ½ tsp ground cumin
- ½ tsp ground coriander
- ½ tsp chilli flakes
- 1 small cinnamon stick
- ½ tsp caster sugar
- Sea salt, to taste

For the fried courgettes
- 500ml (18fl oz) vegetable oil, for frying
- 2 green courgettes, sliced very thinly and kept in salted water
- Plain flour for dusting (about 200g/7oz)

Serves 6–8

This recipe is refreshing and delicious on a hot day. The sliced almonds add great texture and the fried courgettes are simply irresistible. If you don't fancy the fuss with the fried courgettes and almonds, just have the soup simple and easy, as it is.

Put all the soup ingredients in a food processor and blitz. Pass through a fine sieve over a large bowl and keep all the liquid and discard the solids. Season with salt and pepper, transfer to a jug and place in the fridge.

Pour boiling water and some salt over the almonds and soak for 30 minutes. (You can also do this the day before and keep in the fridge in water. Hydrated almonds with sea salt are a great snack all round so if you fancy hydrating more and storing them then do that. They keep well for 2–3 days in the fridge.)

Melt the butter in a small saucepan and simmer gently until it turns golden and smells nutty and sweet. Add the sesame and black onion seeds, all the spices, the sugar and salt. Mix for a couple of minutes and remove from the heat. Remove the cinnamon stick, transfer to a bowl and put to one side.

When you are ready to eat the soup, it's time to fry the courgettes.

Heat the oil in a frying pan over a medium heat. Put the flour in a bowl, take the courgettes out of the water and place them in the flour. Toss them around, making sure they are well coated. Check the oil is hot by lowering in one piece of courgette – it should bubble instantly. Shake excess flour off the courgettes and carefully place them in the oil – don't stir. Allow to cook for a few minutes and then you can start to move them around to make sure they all cook evenly. When they are crunchy and golden, remove from the pan using a slotted spoon and place on kitchen paper to absorb any excess oil.

Serve the soup very chilled or over ice, topped up with hydrated almonds, the spice mix and a handful of crunchy fried courgettes.

Raw Artichokes with Lemon and Oil

Serves 4–6 as a sharing plate

I had never seen artichokes without spikes. My memories of artichokes go hand in hand with other semi-traumatic memories – like bees and nettles. If it wasn't the bees, whose hives were close by, it was the artichokes with their sharp spikes that got me. I thought I was careful and organized when I walked to the artichoke field after lunch. It was the best time of the day as Theía Koula and Theíos Nikos went to sleep for an hour or so after their enormous lunch and a few glasses of red, which, of course, was 'good for you'. I was not allowed to pick artichokes because they were to be saved and cooked with broad beans or lamb when the time was right. I, of course, picked them all the time and thought that I would never get caught. So, after eating my raw artichokes with lemon and salt I used to walk back down to the house where everyone would be awake after their nap. When I was confronted about my doings I confidently denied every time that I had been eating artichokes – with my stained lips and teeth that blatantly gave away exactly what I was doing.

Theía Koula and I would sit on the marble steps that led to her kitchen with a large bucket of water that had in it a handful of salt and 3 or 4 lemons, cut in half, to prepare the artichokes. I was allowed to eat the flesh attached to the end of the inner leaves but not allowed to eat the heart. That was the deal. Sometimes, but very rarely, she would give me a thin slice of the heart and I felt special.

I love raw artichokes. In Crete it's very rare that they are served raw. They are usually cooked with other spring delicacies like broad beans in a white sauce, which usually means no tomato. A bit of carrot, spring onion and dill are classic accompaniments and, of course, lots of lemon.

- 3–4 large artichokes, leaves removed, trimmed and 'choked' (see page 70)
- Juice of 2 lemons
- 50ml (2fl oz) extra virgin olive oil
- Sea salt

Cut the artichokes in half and slice them as thinly as possible. Put them on a plate, season them with salt, lemon juice and olive oil and simply eat them.

I also love eating them with a plate of horta (see page 130) and a nice piece of mature sheep's cheese. Raw artichokes and hard cheese go very well together. Another lovely thing to do with this simple dish is to add some super-fresh raw prawns, peeled, or very thinly sliced raw scallop to create a kind of ceviche. If you do this, marinate the seafood with the artichokes and a bit more lemon juice for 5 minutes before serving.

Artichoke and Broad Bean Stew

Serves 4

This is a classic spring dish. It takes time and patience to prep the artichokes and pod the beans, but it's well worth the effort. If you happen to have some fresh peas around, then add some of those too.

- 4 large fresh artichokes, prepped (see page 70) and only the hearts kept
- 100ml (3½fl oz) extra virgin olive oil
- 2 large white onions, peeled and diced
- 2 large carrots, peeled and diced
- 100ml (3½fl oz) white wine
- 500g (1lb 2oz) fresh broad beans, podded
- 1 bunch of dill, chopped
- 1 bunch of mint leaves, chopped
- Juice of 2 lemons
- Sea salt and freshly ground black pepper, to taste

Cut the artichoke hearts into 6, or 4 if they are smaller. Heat a pan over a medium heat and add the oil, artichokes, onions and carrots to the pan. Cook gently for about 10–15 minutes, or until the onions are soft and translucent.

Add the wine to the pan, cover and cook for another 5 minutes. Check the artichokes and carrots; they should be soft and almost ready. If this is the case, add the broad beans, dill and mint to the pan. Stir and season with salt and pepper. Cook for a few more minutes, add the lemon juice and remove from the heat.

I like this dish as it is, but it also goes really well with slow-cooked lamb if you fancy it.

the LAND

Fava Bean Purée with Quail Eggs

Serves 4

I like to make this at the same time as the Dried Broad Bean Dip on page 106, and keep both of them in the fridge for a few days. I serve them on the same plate because the fava bean purée is light and delicate and the other is rich and intense. The best way to eat these dips is with fried quail eggs and an onion, olive and parsley salsa for the top.

— 200g (7oz) dried Greek fava beans (yellow split peas)
— 1 litre (1¾ pints) water, possibly more
— 2 bay leaves
— ½ white onion, halved
— 150ml (¼ pint) extra virgin olive oil, plus 1 tbsp
— 7 quail eggs
— Sea salt, to taste

For the salsa
— 1 red onion, finely diced
— 1 handful of black olives with their stones removed
— 1 handful of parsley leaves, chopped
— 50ml (2fl oz) extra virgin olive oil
— Juice of 1 lemon
— Sea salt and freshly ground black pepper, to taste

Rinse the fava beans in a sieve under cold water before cooking. The water will initially be cloudy and then turn clear, which means the beans are clean. Tip them into a pan with the water, bay leaves and onion and bring to the boil. Reduce the heat and continue cooking the fava gently for about 30–40 minutes.

When they begin to break up and look almost like a purée, add the 150ml (¼ pint) olive oil and salt, cook for a further 10 minutes or so and remove from the heat. During the last few minutes of cooking the fava, you need to stir regularly so that it does not stick to the bottom of the pan. The more it thickens, the more likely this is to happen.

When the dip is ready, it should be smooth and glossy. Remove the bay leaves, adjust the seasoning and transfer to a dish to cool down. This is a dip that can be eaten hot or cold.

Note: fava beans vary in their cooking time, so keep an eye on the water. You may need to add a little more during the cooking process, but don't add too much or your fava will never thicken.

Heat a flat-bottomed frying pan over a medium heat. When hot, add the tablespoon of olive oil and 'cut' the eggs open using a small serrated knife – don't try to crack them into the pan because the yolk will probably break. Fry the eggs and carefully remove them from the pan to a plate with a spatula.

Just before serving, make the salsa by mixing all of the ingredients together in a bowl. Place the salsa on top of the fava, followed by the eggs.

A Cruciferous Vegetable Salad with Pomegranates

Serves 4–6 as a sharing plate

This recipe brings together vegetables belonging to the brassica family, but the word 'cruciferous' is too good not to use – it refers to the flowers of the plants, which resemble a cross. This salad is simple, crunchy and super punchy. Without the olive oil, it keeps perfectly in the fridge for a few days.

Grate the cauliflower and red and white cabbage using the coarse side of a box grater. Mix all the ingredients in a bowl, adjust the seasoning and serve.

— 200g (7oz) cauliflower
— 200g (7oz) red cabbage
— 200g (7oz) white cabbage
— 1 kohlrabi, peeled and chopped into long strips
— 1 small bunch of radishes, chopped
— 2 carrots, grated
— 200g (7oz) fresh dates, chopped (use dried medjool dates if you can't get hold of fresh)
— Seeds from 1 pomegranate
— 150ml (¼ pint) aged sweet white wine vinegar
— 2 tbsp sugar
— 1 tbsp extra virgin olive oil
— Sea salt to taste

Oven-baked Aubergines with Chickpeas, Spicy Tomatoes and Sheep's Cheese Béchamel

— 3 large aubergines, cut in half
lengthways, scored and lightly
salted

— 3 tbsp extra virgin olive oil

— ½ can good-quality chickpeas
(about 150g/5½oz). Freshly
cooked chickpeas are best;
however, when you only need a
small quantity, canned ones are
an easier option

For the tomato sauce
— 100ml (3½fl oz) olive oil
— 3 red onions, diced
— 400g (14oz) ripe red tomatoes,
blitzed
— ½ cinnamon stick
— 1 red chilli, deseeded and finely
chopped
— Sea salt and freshly ground black
pepper, to taste

For the béchamel
— 70g (2½oz) unsalted butter
— 1 tbsp plain flour
— 200ml (7fl oz) whole milk
— 250g (9oz) mature sheep's
cheese, grated (I use Cretan
Graviera, but you could use
Gruyère or Manchego too)
— ½ nutmeg, grated using the
fine side of a box grater
— Sea salt, to taste

Serves 4–6 as a sharing plate

This is a dish that everyone likes. It's comforting and delicious and the cheesy béchamel over the top just makes it more luxurious. Make sure your aubergines are ripe when you buy them – if they are hard then they will always be a bit bitter and the flesh will never be sweet and silky.

Preheat the oven to 200°C/400°F/gas mark 6.

Place the aubergines on a baking tray and drizzle the olive oil over the top. Cook them in the oven until soft, but not falling apart – this should take about 30 minutes. Remove them from the oven and allow them to cool a little (don't turn off the oven). When they are cool enough to handle, remove half of the flesh from each half using a spoon and place in a bowl. Add the chickpeas to the bowl. Set aside the aubergine shells.

To make the tomato sauce, heat a small pan and add the olive oil together with the onions. Cook for a few minutes until the onions become translucent and sweet. Add all the remaining ingredients to the pan, cover with a lid, and turn down the heat. Allow the sauce to cook for about 20–25 minutes or until nice and sweet. Remove the cinnamon stick and set the pan aside.

Making the béchamel is super fast. Melt the butter in a small pan and, when golden, whisk in the flour. Keep whisking for a minute and add the milk, followed by the cheese and nutmeg. It will take about 2 minutes to thicken. Remove from the heat and check the seasoning.

Mix the tomato sauce with the chickpeas and aubergine flesh and check the seasoning. Place the aubergine shells back on a baking tray and stuff them carefully. Pour the cheesy béchamel over the top and place in the hot oven for about 25 minutes or until golden and piping hot.

the LAND

AEGEAN

Beetroot Salad with Yogurt, Carob Molasses and Almonds

Serves 4–6 as a sharing plate

I love beetroot and this salad is so good. Adding carob molasses and vinegar to the dressing makes the salad sweet but punchy at the same time. The almonds add a great crunch and the yogurt just brings everything together. Make sure you get firm, freshly picked beetroot as you don't want the strong, earthy flavour old beetroot gives.

— 6 medium beetroot
— 1 handful of fresh mint leaves, chopped
— 1 tbsp chopped dill
— 100g (3½oz) raw almonds, soaked in boiling water for 1 hour
— 1 garlic clove, crushed to a paste with a bit of salt
— 50ml (2fl oz) carob molasses (grape or date molasses will also work well)
— 2 tbsp good-quality red wine vinegar
— 2 tbsp olive oil
— 100g (3½fl oz) Greek strained yogurt
— Sea salt, to taste

Boil the beetroot in a pan of water until soft. Drain, allow to cool, then peel and slice into thin wedges. Put the beetroot in a serving bowl together with the herbs and almonds.

Make the dressing by shaking the crushed garlic, molasses, vinegar and olive oil in a jar; pour over the beetroot and mix. Season with salt.

Add the yogurt to the salad and mix slightly. The colour of this is amazing if you don't fully mix in the yogurt.

Trahana Soup with Dried Mint and Deep-fried Cheese

Serves 4

Alex, my husband, loves this soup. He actually introduced me to it, but he usually makes it with chicken. It's a perfect pick-me-up when you are feeling a bit under the weather. The addition of the mint sauce and chilli butter, together with the fried feta, makes it a treat when you need a quick simple soup.

Trahana (dried, fermented wheat with sheep's milk) can be bought in Greek and Turkish shops, but when I can't get hold of it, I make a similar version with soaked bulgur wheat mixed with yogurt and dried in a very low oven. This is definitely not the real thing, but it's quite fun to make and you can add lots of dried herbs and spices to it too.

— 200g (7oz) trahana
— 2 litres (3½ pints) water (you might need a little more)
— 2 garlic cloves, peeled
— 1 white onion, chopped
— 1 small bunch of fresh mint, stalks discarded
— 40ml (1½fl oz) extra virgin olive oil
— 1 tsp dried mint
— 50g (1¾oz) butter
— 2 tsp Turkish chilli flakes
— 200g (7oz) feta, cut into cubes
— 200ml (7fl oz) vegetable oil, for frying
— Plain flour, for dusting
— 1 organic egg, beaten
— Sea salt and freshly ground black pepper, to taste

Soak the trahana in 1 litre (1¾ pints) of cold water for 1 hour. Transfer to a pot and add another litre (1¾ pints) of water, the garlic and the onion. Cook over a medium heat for about 40 minutes until the trahana has broken up and the soup begins to thicken. Stir the base of the pot occasionally to prevent sticking. Add a little more water, if necessary. Taste the soup – the trahana should feel soft. Season with salt and remove from the heat. I like to blitz the soup as I think it looks nicer and silkier, but there is no need to do so.

In the meantime, blitz the mint leaves with the olive oil and dried mint until smooth. Put in a bowl and season with salt.

Make the chilli butter by caramelizing the butter in a small pan until golden and then adding the chilli flakes. The butter will froth a bit when you add the chilli, so make sure the pan you are using has enough space to allow for this. Overflowing chilli butter is dangerous and no fun to clean. Remove from the heat and keep the chilli butter in a warm place to remain liquid. If it sets, then gently warm it up again before serving.

When you are ready to serve, fry the feta cheese. Heat the oil until hot but not smoking. Roll the feta in flour, then in the egg and back into the flour. Gently drop in the hot oil and fry until golden (it should bubble instantly if the oil is hot enough). Remove and place on kitchen paper for a minute.

Serve the soup with some of the mint sauce and chilli butter on the top and cubes of crispy fried feta.

the LAND

Chicken, Squash and Feta Fritters with Mint, Black Olives, Walnuts and Crispy Sage

Serves 4–6 as a sharing plate

I usually make fritters without meat, but these are so good I had to share them. I have included chicken in this recipe, but guinea fowl works wonderfully too, if you can find it. These fritters are creamy, with the olives and walnuts adding a saltiness and texture that is so good.

— 2 tbsp extra virgin olive oil, plus extra for coating
— 1 large white onion, diced
— 200g (7oz) organic chicken fillets, skin off
— 300g (10½oz) butternut squash, peeled, grated coarsely and lightly salted
— 100g (3½oz) bulgur wheat, soaked in hot water
— 100g (3½oz) feta cheese, crumbled
— 2 tbsp black olives, pitted and chopped finely
— 1 tbsp walnuts, chopped finely
— 1 large handful of mint leaves, chopped
— 2 organic eggs
— 2 small handfuls of plain flour, plus extra for dusting
— 200–300ml (7–10fl oz) vegetable oil, for frying
— 1 handful of sage leaves
— Sea salt and freshly ground black pepper, to taste

Heat a small pan, add 1 tablespoon of oil and the onions. Cook until translucent and sweet.

Heat the remaining olive oil in another pan. Season the chicken fillets with salt and coat them with some olive oil. Pan fry them for a few minutes, turning regularly, until cooked. Shred and put them to one side.

Squeeze the excess water from the butternut squash and put in a bowl with the onion, drained bulgur, feta, olives, walnuts and mint.

Add the eggs, flour and chicken and give everything a really good mix. Adjust the seasoning. The mix should be quite wet but manageable. Shape into large walnut-sized balls.

Heat the oil until hot but not smoking – check by adding a sage leaf, which should bubble instantly. Before you fry the fritters, drop the sage leaves into the oil for a minute or two to crisp them up. Remove and drain on kitchen paper.

Roll the balls of mix in the flour and fry until golden, then remove and drain on kitchen paper. Sprinkle the sage leaves on top of the fritters and serve.

Fresh Corn with Parsley and Chilli with Strained Yogurt and Fried Crispbreads

Serves 4–6 as a sharing plate

Strained yogurt is a great dip. Hanging Greek yogurt overnight makes it really thick and it basically becomes a good-quality cream cheese with just the right acidity. The buttered corn is simply delicious and the crispbreads are so easy to make. Both the yogurt ball and the crispbreads last for a few days in airtight containers in the fridge.

— 3 corn on the cob
— 1 handful of parsley, chopped as finely as possible
— 50g (1¾oz) goat's butter
— 30g (1oz) unsalted butter
— 1 tsp Turkish chilli flakes

For the strained yogurt
— 250g (9oz) Greek yogurt
— 2 tsp fine sea salt
— 1 tbsp Turkish chilli flakes
— 1 tsp dried dill
— 3 tbsp walnuts, crushed finely
— 100ml (3½fl oz) extra virgin olive oil

For the crispbreads
— 200g (7oz) plain flour
— 2 tsp extra virgin olive oil
— 100ml (3½fl oz) tepid water
— 1 tbsp black onion seeds
— 100ml (3½fl oz) vegetable oil, for frying
— Sea salt, to taste

Put the yogurt in a bowl with the salt, chilli flakes and dried dill. Mix very well. You will need to hang this overnight to make it nice and thick — a bit like cream cheese. Line a bowl with a large cheesecloth or another type of cloth and pour the yogurt mix into the bowl. Pull the sides of the cloth together and tie a knot just above the yogurt mix. Hang this using a hook wherever works with a bowl underneath to collect the liquid.

When the yogurt is ready (it will be firm to the touch and the bowl will have quite a bit of liquid), remove it from the cloth and place it in a bowl. Take walnut-sized quantities and roll between your palms to make small balls, then roll in the walnuts and place on a flat dish. When you have rolled all the mix, pour over the olive oil so it covers the balls.

For the crispbreads, add the flour to a bowl with the olive oil and salt. Add the water slowly — you may not need all of it — to combine the mixture to a smooth dough. Work the dough on a flat surface for a few minutes and put to one side. It should be silky and elastic.

Boil the corn in a pan of salted water for about 40 minutes. Remove from the water and, using a sharp knife, cut the kernels off the cob. Mix with the parsley and put to one side.

Heat both butters in a pan and, when golden brown, add the chilli flakes. Be careful as the butter will froth up, so make sure your pan is large enough for this to happen. Stir for a minute, then pour over the corn and parsley.

Roll the dough out quite thinly on a floured surface. Make sure you can lift it up easily without tearing. Cut the dough into wonky triangles, sprinkle some black onion seeds and press them down gently so they stick to the dough.

Heat the oil to fry the crispbreads. The oil needs to be hot, but not too hot, otherwise they will burn before they are cooked. Check the oil by adding a small bit of dough – it should bubble gently. Fry in the oil for about 2 minutes or until golden on both sides. Remove and drain on kitchen paper.

To serve, arrange the crispbreads and corn on a board or plate and finish with the strained yogurt balls.

AEGEAN

Horta – Blanched Greens with Olive Oil, Lemon, Chopped Tomato and Garlic

— 1kg (2lb 4oz) wild greens

— 3 tbsp extra virgin olive oil

— Juice of 1–2 lemons (depending on size, juiciness and personal preference)

— 1 large red tomato, grated

— 1 garlic clove, finely diced

— Sea salt, to taste

Serves 4–6 as a sharing plate

Horta refers to both wild and cultivated greens that are usually boiled and eaten with olive oil and lemon. They are a staple in our diet and, as the types change according to the seasons, you come to crave a sweet plate of 'vlita' (amaranth) in summer or the more bitter 'radikia' (dandelions) and 'askrolympous' (Spanish oyster thistle) in winter. Crete has dozens of varieties: mustard leaves, endive, sorrel, wild fennel, nettles, wild leeks and wild asparagus are some of the most common. The hard bit comes when you go out foraging for all the other kinds that only some people recognize. This amazing skill develops after years of foraging.

When I think of wild greens, many images come to mind. As I grew up, all the ladies in the neighbourhood would set off with their baskets and knife to return after hours with a basketful of delicious muddy greens. However, the most powerful image is that of a lady who sells her foraged greens at the weekly street market. I could not have been more than 5 years old when I used to go with my mum to the market to do the restaurant shopping. That's when I first met her. She was small with long brown hair, but the strongest woman I had ever met. Her hands were big and had worked hard and her voice was deep and powerful. She moved crates around as if they were feather pillows and her stall was the smallest one, but the most eye-catching. She had very few things to sell, but her two hands had sourced them all. Her face looked tired even then. Thirty years later and every time I visit Chania I go to the same market. Lots of things have changed but she is still there, doing exactly the same thing. I look at her even more tired face and I respect the knowledge that soul holds.

The recipe here states wild greens. In the UK and elsewhere, you can use wild nettles, garlic leaves, chickweed, garlic mustard or wild fennel. If you can't get your hands on wild greens, then use spinach, dill and chard in equal quantities.

Bring a large pot of water to the boil – it must be big enough to fit the greens loosely. In the meantime, wash the greens thoroughly by dunking them in a bucket of cold water and 1 tablespoon of salt. Make sure all the soil has been washed off otherwise you will feel the grittiness when you eat them. Drop the greens into the boiling water and make sure they are all submerged. Cook until the stems are tender and soft. Remove from the pot using a slotted spoon and spread out on a clean cloth to cool a little.

Transfer to a bowl and season with oil, lemon juice and salt. Put the grated tomato and garlic on top and eat immediately. I enjoy eating them with a plate of pickled 'volvi', edible bulbs that are a Cretan delicacy. 'Volvi' are similar to onions, wild and take years to reach maturity. They are quite bitter, hard to extract from the earth and need ages to pickle, but they are amazing to eat.

AEGEAN

the LAND

Stuffed Vine Leaves with Rice and Carrots

6–8 as a sharing plate

These stuffed vine leaves – or dolmas – are delicious hot or cold and usually served with a big dollop of thick Greek yogurt.

- 200g (7oz) carrots, coarsely grated
- 300g (10½oz) tomatoes, blitzed
- 120g (4¼oz) round (short-grain) rice
- 1 handful of parsley, chopped
- 2 handfuls of mint, chopped
- 1 handful of dill, chopped
- 100ml (3½fl oz) olive oil, plus a little extra
- 1 tsp dried oregano
- Juice of 1 lemon
- Sea salt and freshly ground black pepper, to taste

- 20–30 good-quality preserved vine leaves, or fresh ones if you can get them

Preheat the oven to 180°C/350°F/gas mark 4.

Put all the ingredients except the vine leaves in a bowl and mix well. The mix needs to be highly seasoned and punchy because it will mellow during cooking.

Preserved vine leaves are usually packed rolled, in jars, so start by separating the leaves carefully so as not to tear them. If you come across small or broken ones you can patch them up using more leaves.

Use a large plate or another flat surface and open one leaf flat. Place a small spoonful of the rice mix in the centre and cover with one part of the leaf, then bring both sides in and roll to seal. Repeat with the rest of the filling and all of the leaves. Place the dolmas on a baking tray, ideally in a single layer with the loose end facing down.

Pour any liquid that accumulates in the plate into the tray as it will add moisture and flavour. Add a splash of water to the tray and a drizzle of oil, cover with baking parchment and then kitchen foil and place in the hot oven. Let the dolmas cook for 30–40 minutes and remove the parchment and foil. The rice should be ready at this point. Cook for another 10 minutes to get some colour on the top and then remove from the oven.

Borlotti Beans, Grilled Vegetables, Quail Eggs and Whipped Feta

Serves 4–6 as a sharing plate

Fresh borlotti beans are simply delicious. I like everything about them – podding them, cooking them and, of course, eating them. It is not often that you get beans in their fresh form and when they are dried they take ages to cook, so getting hold of fresh ones is a luxury in any kitchen.

For the whipped feta
- 100g (3½oz) good-quality feta
- 1 tsp extra virgin olive oil
- 1 tbsp water
- ½ tsp sugar

For the beans
- 1kg (2lb 4oz) fresh borlotti beans, podded weight
- 1 cinnamon stick
- 2 bay leaves
- 250g (9oz) ripe tomatoes, chopped
- 4 sprigs of lemon thyme
- 50ml (2fl oz) extra virgin olive oil
- 1 litre (1¾ pints) water

For the grilled vegetables and wilted herbs
- 1 red onion, unpeeled
- 1 red horn pepper
- 1 aubergine, pierced a few times with a sharp knife
- 1 tbsp extra virgin olive oil
- 1 tbsp aged red wine vinegar
- 2 handfuls of spinach, chopped
- 1 handful of dill, chopped
- Sea salt, to taste

- 10 quail eggs
- Fresh mint leaves, chopped, to finish

Make the whipped feta first by blitzing all the ingredients together until smooth and silky. Transfer to a bowl and place in the fridge until needed.

To cook the beans, place everything in a pan and cook gently over a medium heat until the beans are soft and the sauce has emulsified. This should take about 40 minutes.

Preheat the oven to 180°C/350°F/gas mark 4. Place the onion, pepper and aubergine on a baking tray, and cover with baking parchment. Cook for about 25–30 minutes or until the vegetables are soft. Remove from the oven and, when they are cool enough to handle, peel the skins off the vegetables and roughly chop or tear them by hand. Put in a bowl and season with the oil, vinegar and salt. Put the spinach and dill in another bowl and season lightly with salt. Using your palms and fingers, gently massage the herbs for a couple of minutes to wilt them.

Boil the quail eggs for 2 minutes, put immediately in iced water, then peel.

When you are ready to serve, pile the beans on a plate and place the seasoned grilled vegetables on top, followed by the wilted herbs, boiled eggs and whipped feta.

Finish the dish with the freshly chopped mint leaves.

the MOUNTAINS

Giant Beans with Celery and Smoked Pork Belly

Serves 4–6 as a sharing plate

I love giant beans (otherwise known as butter or elephant beans). I spend a lot of time searching for good-quality pulses. Finding ones that are not too old and have been grown and preserved well makes a massive difference to how they respond to cooking as well as flavour. I came across a man in the north of Greece who mainly cultivates them for his personal use, but had had a great harvest and sent me a few kilos to try. They were soft, buttery and almost tasted of chestnuts. I had some beautiful smoked pork belly from Kent and made this dish, which is perfect on a chilly day with lots of fresh bread to mop up the juices.

- 350g (12oz) dried giant beans (also known as butter or elephant beans)
- 100ml (3½fl oz) extra virgin olive oil, plus 1 tbsp
- 2 garlic cloves, peeled but kept whole
- 2 medium white onions, diced
- 1kg (2lb 4oz) leafy celery, chopped
- 4 carrots, diced
- 4 bay leaves
- 3 rosemary sprigs, leaves finely chopped
- 300g (10½oz) smoked pork belly, chopped into bite-sized pieces
- 200ml (7fl oz) white wine
- 1 handful of parsley, chopped
- 1 handful of dill, chopped
- Juice of 3 lemons

Soak the beans overnight in lots of water.

The following day, drain and place them in a large pot with enough fresh water to cover them by about 5cm (2in) and add the 1 tablespoon of olive oil. Bring the beans to the boil and add the garlic, onions, celery, carrots, bay and rosemary to the pot. Cook over a medium heat for about 30 minutes. Add the pork belly to the pot together with the wine and continue cooking for about another 1 hour. The beans should begin to soften and some of them will break up, making the dish quite creamy. The pork belly should also be tender, but if you need to, cook gently for longer to achieve this – the time can vary a lot, depending on the quality of the beans you are using.

When you are happy with the textures, add the remaining olive oil, parsley, dill and lemon juice to the pot, give it a stir and turn the heat off. Let the beans sit for a while before serving.

This dish will only get better with time, so any leftovers will be perfect for the next couple of days.

Thyme, Oregano and Fenugreek Pork Fillet with Tsatziki, Tomato and Onion Salad

Serves 4

- 1 pork fillet (about 500g/1lb 2oz)
- A little extra virgin olive oil, if pan frying

For the spice mix
- 1 tsp dried thyme
- 1 tsp dried oregano
- 1 tsp black pepper
- 1 tsp Turkish chilli flakes
- 1 tsp ground fenugreek
- 1 tsp smoked hot paprika
- Sea salt, to taste (be generous)

For the tsatziki
- 1 cucumber, grated on the coarse side of a box grater, and salted
- 200g (7oz) Greek yogurt
- 2 garlic cloves, crushed into a paste with a touch of salt
- 1 tsp red wine vinegar
- 3 tbsp extra virgin olive oil

For the tomato and onion salad
- 2 ripe red tomatoes, halved and thinly sliced
- 1 red onion, halved and thinly sliced
- 1 tsp dried oregano
- Juice of 1 lemon
- 1 tbsp extra virgin olive oil
- Sea salt and freshly ground black pepper, to taste

I started using fenugreek after visiting Turkey a few years ago. I did not know what it was, how to include it in my cooking, what the plant looked like. I recognized the flavour in pastourma, but have never tasted it in anything else. I had it in Turkey with cured fish (see page 66) and I was blown away. Together with other spices it is used to make a paste known as 'çemen' in Turkish and 'tsimeni' in Greek, rubbed onto meat and fish as part of the cure. In recent years I have experimented a lot with fenugreek seeds and have included them in stews, marinades and, of course, curing pastes.

In Crete, oregano, salt and pepper are mostly used for grilled meats. The addition of hot and aromatic spices is not very common. I added some fenugreek powder to this simple seasoning and I must say that I will never cook pork on the grill without it again.

I prefer to cook the pork fillet on a charcoal grill because the flavour is better when you use fire, but you can pan-fry it with a touch of olive oil.

Combine the ingredients for the spice mix and rub it over the pork fillet and let it sit for at least 30 minutes. Make sure your pan is hot before you add the oil and the fillet. Brown it all over and then lower the heat to the minimum. Continue cooking for about 8–10 minutes until it feels quite firm to the touch. I like having this slightly pink, but not underdone. When the fillet is ready, remove from the heat and let it rest for at least 10 minutes. Slice thinly.

Squeeze the salted cucumber to get rid of the excess water and place in a bowl together with all the other tsatziki ingredients. Stir, check the seasoning and put to one side.

Quickly make the tomato salad by mixing everything in a bowl. Check the seasoning.

Serve by putting slices of pork, accompanied by some tsatziki and tomato salad, on a flat plate.

Slow-cooked Rabbit with Whole Baby Onions and Hazelnut and Parsley Sauce

— 100ml (3½fl oz) extra virgin olive oil
— 1kg (2lb 4oz) rabbit, cut into 6–8 pieces
— 1kg (2lb 4oz) white small onions, peeled, but kept whole
— 1kg ripe red tomatoes, blitzed in a food processor
— 1 cinnamon stick
— 4 bay leaves
— Juice and zest of 1 unwaxed orange
— 300ml red wine

For the hazelnut and parsley sauce
— 2 handfuls of parsley, chopped
— 1 tbsp olive oil
— 2 tbsp roasted, chopped hazelnuts
— 1 tsp red wine vinegar
— Sea salt, to taste

Serves 4–6 as a sharing plate

This is an all-time favourite. As a kid, I was not very fond of rabbit, but have grown to absolutely love it. My Theía Koula used to have her own rabbits on her little farm and used to cook them often. I remember my brother and I returning from school and, as soon as he realized she had cooked rabbit, he forgot about mum's lunch and went straight downstairs and sat at Theía Koula's kitchen table, waiting to be served a nice plate of rabbit stew.

Heat the olive oil in a large pan and season the rabbit with salt. When the oil is hot, but not smoking, add the rabbit and brown the pieces on both sides. When the meat is golden, add the onions, tomatoes, cinnamon, bay leaves, orange zest and juice and wine. Stir and bring to the boil. Lower the heat, cover with a lid and let it simmer for about 45 minutes or until the rabbit is cooked and tender and the sauce is thick and delicious. If you think the sauce is evaporating too fast you can add a small glass of water to the pan. When ready, turn off the heat and let the rabbit rest for 15–20 minutes.

Meanwhile, make the hazelnut and parsley sauce in a pestle and mortar. Crush the parsley with some salt and the tablespoon of olive oil until it looks like a bright green sauce. Add the hazelnuts, vinegar and season with salt.

Serve on top of the rabbit with some slices of fresh bread to mop up the juices.

AEGEAN

Fried Rabbit with Rosemary and Vinegar

Serves 4–6 as a sharing plate

Traditionally this is a dish known as 'savori', which involves frying with rosemary and vinegar. You can make it with fish or meat – at home my dad used to cook this when he caught a big moray eel. (He could never sell them at the market or in the restaurant so we usually ate them at home.) It involves dusting the fish or meat in flour and frying it in olive oil with lots of rosemary chopped into it. When it's ready, you pour some good-quality vinegar over it and turn the heat off.

In this recipe using rabbit the rosemary sauce is made separately. This gives you more control over the sauce and it's easier to make sure it has the right sweetness and saltiness. If you want to try it with another meat such as chicken or pork, or fish such as mackerel or anchovies, feel free to do so – it will be delicious.

— 150g (5½oz) plain flour
— 1kg (2lb 4oz) rabbit, cut into
   6–8 pieces
— 200ml (7fl oz) olive oil, for frying
— Sea salt, to taste

For the rosemary sauce
— 3 tbsp roughly chopped
   rosemary
— 2–3 tbsp aged sweet white
   wine vinegar
— 3 tbsp extra virgin olive oil
— 1 tsp sugar

To make the rosemary sauce, blitz 2 tablespoons of the rosemary with the vinegar, the olive oil and the sugar in a food processor. A pestle and mortar will also work but it will take a bit more time. Pour into a bowl and season with salt.

To fry the rabbit, put the flour in a bowl and mix it with ½ teaspoon of fine sea salt and the remaining tablespoon of chopped rosemary. Toss the rabbit pieces in the flour and shake off any excess. Pour the oil into a large saucepan and set over a medium heat. When the oil is hot, but not smoking, gently place the rabbit pieces into the oil and fry until golden and crispy on both sides. Check that the meat is cooked through, but juicy and soft. Remove from the oil with a slotted spoon and place in a bowl lined with kitchen paper to absorb any excess oil.

Sprinkle over some salt and toss gently. Arrange on a plate and serve immediately with the rosemary sauce spooned on top. You don't need to heat the sauce – simply use it as a dressing.

the MOUNTAINS

Chicken with Okra, Oregano and Aged Vinegar

- 700g (1lb 9oz) okra, stems trimmed as little as possible
- 2 tsp vinegar, any kind will do
- 50ml (2fl oz) extra virgin olive oil
- 800g (1lb 12oz) chicken on the bone, skin removed, cut into small pieces
- 400g (14oz) can good-quality chopped tomatoes
- 1 tbsp sun-dried tomatoes, chopped
- 2 tsp dried oregano
- 1 tsp freshly ground black pepper
- 100ml (3½fl oz) red wine
- 500ml (18fl oz) water
- 1 tbsp aged red wine vinegar
- Sea salt, to taste

Serves 4–6 as a sharing plate

Okra, or ladies' fingers, is usually slimy when cooked and there is nothing worse than slimy okra. Growing up in Halepa, I remember the ladies in the neighbourhood laying out massive trays of okra in the sun to dry. They used to toss the okra in some vinegar and leave them in the hot sun to get rid of the sliminess. I loved the sight of extra-long shiny silver trays crammed with long, short, fat, thin and wonky ladies' fingers. I think the acid in the vinegar must disintegrate or do something chemically to the sliminess so I always follow their method. Since the sun is not always around in England, I use the oven to dry them out.

Preheat the oven to 150°C/300°F/gas mark 2.

Put the okra on a tray and toss with the vinegar. Put in the oven for about 20–30 minutes until they start to dry out. Remove and put to one side.

Increase the oven temperature to 200°C/400°F/gas mark 6.

Heat the oil in a large saucepan and season the chicken generously with salt. Brown the pieces on both sides until golden – this should take about 10 minutes. Add all the other ingredients, including the okra, to the pan, give them all a stir and cover with a lid.

Cook gently for about 30 minutes or until the chicken is almost cooked. Transfer the chicken and okra from the pan into an oven dish and finish the cooking in the oven. This last stage should take about 20 minutes and will make some of the okra chewy and concentrated in flavour and crisp up the chicken, which makes the dish even more delicious.

Slow-Cooked Pork in Apple Juice with Malotira, Chickpea Purée and Leek and Parsley Sauce

- 800g–1kg pork (12oz–2lb 4oz) shoulder, off the bone, kept in one piece if possible
- 400–500ml (14–18fl oz) good-quality apple juice
- 1 small handful of dried malotira (Cretan mountain tea)
- 1 tbsp dried throubi
- 2 tsp freshly ground black pepper
- 2 tsp smoked sweet paprika
- 2 tsp dried oregano
- 6 sage leaves
- 2 tbsp extra virgin olive oil
- Sea salt, to taste

For the purée
- 3 tbsp extra virgin olive oil
- 1 garlic clove, chopped
- 1 small white onion, finely diced
- 400g (14oz) can cooked chickpeas, rinsed and drained
- Sea salt, to taste

For the sauce
- 2 tbsp extra virgin olive oil
- 2 garlic cloves, chopped
- 1 large leek, trimmed and finely sliced
- 1 bunch of parsley, chopped
- 1 tbsp tahini
- Sea salt and freshly ground black pepper, to taste

Serves 4–6 as a sharing plate

Using Cretan herbs for this dish is wonderful. Malotira is mostly used for tea and has a plethora of medicinal properties. Using it as seasoning gives the dish an interesting mountain aroma and an earthiness that's delicious. Throubi is another wild herb often used to season meat and is best known as summer savory. If these herbs are unavailable, use more oregano and sage instead. Both the sauce and purée can be made in advance and reheated or served chilled.

This is amazing in flatbreads or a bun too. It's a bit like a souvlaki, but with a different flavour combination. I love making the flatbreads and layering them with the creamy chickpeas, leek sauce and chunks of aromatic pork. They make a great wrap to eat in or out.

Place the pork in an ovenproof dish and cover with the apple juice. Refrigerate overnight.

The following day, preheat the oven to 180–200°C/350–400°F/gas mark 4–6. Take the pork out of the apple juice, rub it with all the dried herbs and spices, season it with salt and put it back in the dish and add 2 tablespoons of olive oil. Cover the dish and cook in the preheated oven for about 1½ hours, or until the pork is tender and juicy. You may need to turn it a few times while cooking to prevent parts of it drying out.

For the chickpea purée, heat a small pan over a medium heat and, after a minute or so, add the oil, garlic and onion and cook until golden. Add the chickpeas and season with salt. Cook for another 10 minutes, remove from the heat and blitz until smooth.

To make the sauce, heat a pan over a medium heat and when hot add the oil, garlic and leek and cook gently for about 20 minutes until the leeks are sweet and translucent. Add the parsley and tahini and remove from the heat. Season with salt and pepper. The leeks should be creamy and glossy, so add a splash of water, if necessary. Blitz the sauce until smooth.

When ready to serve, pull the pork apart and serve it with the purée and leek sauce on the side. Make sure you pour some of the sauces collected in the baking dish all over it.

Grilled Quail with Aubergine and Graviera

Serves 4

I started eating quail in England and loved it. It's super-easy to cook and its flavour is not as strong as most game. Whether you throw it on a charcoal grill, cook it in a pan or deep-fry it, it's just one of the best small birds around.

Marinate the quail with the salt, pepper, cinnamon, juniper berries and molasses and place in the fridge until needed.

Heat the olive oil in a small pan and add the garlic, rosemary, thyme and bay leaves. When the garlic is golden, add the tomatoes and cook for another 5 minutes. Add the aubergines to the pan and season with salt. Cover with a lid and cook gently until everything is soft and sweet. This should take about 20–25 minutes. Add the vinegar and cook for a couple more minutes. Add the Graviera and milk and stir well until the cheese has melted. Remove from the heat and stir in the mint.

If you have a charcoal grill on the go that would be perfect. Grill the birds over a medium heat for about 6–7 minutes on each side or longer if you like the meat well done. If you don't have a charcoal grill, then brown the birds in a pan with a touch of olive oil and then finish cooking them in an oven preheated to 180°C/350°F/gas mark 4 for about 12 minutes.

To serve, heat up the aubergine sauce, ladle onto plates and put the quail on top. Serve with some freshly cut lemon wedges.

For the quail
- 4 quail (spatchcocked)
- 1 tsp sea salt
- 1 tsp freshly ground black pepper
- 1 tsp ground cinnamon
- 1 tsp crushed juniper berries
- 4 tbsp grape molasses

- 2 tbsp extra virgin olive oil
- 1 small head of new season garlic or 4 garlic cloves, crushed
- 1 tbsp fresh rosemary, chopped
- 1 tbsp fresh lemon thyme, chopped
- 3 bay leaves
- 200g (7oz) tomatoes, finely chopped
- 2 aubergines, diced/cubed
- 1 tbsp aged sweet white wine vinegar
- 2 tbsp grated Cretan Graviera (or another mature sheep's milk cheese such as Gruyère or Manchego)
- 100ml (3½fl oz) milk
- 2 tbsp roughly chopped fresh mint leaves
- Sea salt, to season
- Lemon wedges, to serve

AEGEAN

Fried Snails with Rosemary Vinegar and Red Wine

- 1kg (2lb 4oz) live snails
- 200ml (7fl oz) olive oil
- Flour, for dusting
- 4 fresh rosemary sprigs
- 150ml (¼ pint) good-quality red wine
- 4 tbsp red wine vinegar
- Sea salt, to taste

Serves 4–6 as a sharing plate

When I go to Crete and want to eat snails, I either visit the market and buy a bag or I go on a long drive to one of the many small villages in the mountains and sit at a traditional kafenio. A kafenio serves coffee, but the majority of them will serve very good raki and the best mezze – small dishes – to accompany your little glass of the devilish drink.

When I was young, however, my Theía Koula would go and collect her own snails when the season was right. She would pop the snails in an old beehive and feed them flour and dried pasta for a few days before cooking them. She said that they needed to clean themselves up as she did not know what they had eaten in the wild. She would then soak them in water for a while and pop them in a pot with tomatoes, potatoes and courgettes. The stew had the most delicate aroma and flavour and Theíos Nikos, her husband, spent hours teaching me how to get them out their shells with a fork. He always said: 'Be patient and delicate and let the fork do the job' and: 'Marianna, always pinch their bum off, it's not clean'. I still pinch their bum off even though many have told me it's the best bit.

This recipe is another Cretan way to eat snails. I love them like this as the flavours are punchy and the eating messier.

Put the snails in a bowl of cold water and let them sit for 1 hour. As they are alive they will start moving around and climb up the bowl, so make sure you keep an eye on them. Boil a pot of water and add some salt. Put the snails in the boiling water and cook for 15–20 minutes. Remove with a slotted spoon and put to one side; discard the water.

Heat the olive oil in a frying pan large enough to hold the snails in a single layer. Dust them with flour. Not much flour will stick on their shells but that's fine; it will help to thicken the sauce a bit. When the oil is hot, but not smoking, add the rosemary then the snails. Don't move them around too much as you want the flour that has stuck to them to stay in place. After a few minutes cooking on one side, turn them and make sure they are golden all over. Add the wine to the pan followed by the vinegar and continue to cook for a few more minutes until the sauce thickens a little. Turn the heat off and transfer the snails to a platter. Add as much or as little of the sauce as you wish. Serve with fresh bread and a nice glass of red wine.

Roasted Lamb Breast with Spicy Feta Sauce

Serves 4–6 as a sharing plate

This is just delicious. I never thought of using feta as a marinade ingredient, but the result is simply amazing. The saltiness and acidity from the cheese make the sauce so moreish you just keep going back for more.

Preheat the oven to 180°C/350°F/gas mark 4.

Blitz all the marinade ingredients until they turn into a paste in a food processor. Pour over the lamb breasts and massage the marinade into the meat. Add any extra on the inside of the breasts and roll them up as you would a mat. At this point you can use some string or wooden skewers to hold them together, but don't worry if you don't have any to hand.

Place the breasts in a deep roasting tin and add enough water to reach about 1cm (½in) up the tray. Cover the tray with baking parchment, tucking in the sides. You don't want to lose too much liquid during the cooking or the sauce will dry out too soon and you will need to add more water. I have two identical trays and I use the second one as a lid over the parchment.

Place in the oven and cook for about 1½–2 hours. Remove the lamb from the oven and check that it is cooked and buttery soft. If it is, remove the paper and lid (if you had one) and continue cooking for another 10–15 minutes until nice and golden on the top.

The sauce is absolutely delicious and super savoury. You can serve the lamb as it is with a nice salad or layer into a bun with some yogurt and some crunchy cucumber.

- 2 lamb breasts, about 1–1.2kg (2lb 4oz–2lb 8oz), deboned by your butcher

For the marinade/sauce
- 1 long green pepper, deseeded and chopped
- 1 long red romano pepper, deseeded and chopped
- 5 red chillies, deseeded and chopped
- 1 handful of mint leaves
- 150g (5½oz) feta
- 1 tsp smoked sweet paprika
- 1 tsp ground cumin
- 1 tsp ground coriander
- 2 tsp Turkish chilli flakes
- 50ml (2fl oz) extra virgin olive oil
- Juice of 1 lemon
- 1 tsp sea salt or to taste

Lamb Kofte with Parsley Salad

Serves 4–6 as a sharing plate

Usually in Crete, we call these 'keftedes' – small meatballs, deep-fried until crispy and served with lots of onion; they are a perfect snack to take to the beach, especially if there are children around. In Turkey, they add bulgur wheat and lots of aromatic spices. The bulgur gives them a great crunch and the spices make them even more tasty. I add a few lambs' hearts in there to intensify the flavour, but omit them if you prefer.

— 1 tbsp extra virgin olive oil
— 150g (5½oz) lambs' hearts, chopped extremely finely and seasoned with salt
— 450g (1lb) lamb, minced
— 100g (3½oz) coarse bulgur wheat
— 1 tbsp walnuts, very finely chopped
— 150g (5½oz) tomatoes, finely chopped
— 2 long green Turkish chillies, or other chillies you like, chopped finely
— 1 tsp freshly ground black pepper
— 1 tsp ground cumin
— 1 tsp dried chilli flakes
— 1½ tsp ground fenugreek
— 1 handful each of parsley, mint leaves and dill, all finely chopped
— 300ml (½ pint) vegetable oil, for frying

For the parsley salad
— 1 bunch of parsley, chopped
— 100g (3½oz) tomatoes, chopped
— 1 small green pepper, deseeded and chopped
— 1 green chilli, deseeded and chopped
— 1 tbsp extra virgin olive oil
— Juice of 1 lemon
— Sea salt and freshly ground black pepper, to taste

Heat a pan over a medium heat, add the oil and lambs' hearts and fry briefly for a couple of minutes. Transfer to a bowl and allow to cool a little.

Tip the bulgur wheat into a bowl, cover with boiling water and let it sit for a few minutes until it softens a little.

Put all the ingredients, except the oil, in a large bowl and mix very well. Season with salt and form into round balls about the size of a walnut.

Heat the vegetable oil in a deep saucepan until hot (the oil should bubble as soon as you lower the kofte into it). Fry the lamb kofte in the oil until golden and crispy. Remove from the pan and drain on kitchen paper.

You need to chop the parsley salad ingredients as finely as possible. Put the parsley, tomatoes, pepper and chilli on a cutting board. Go over them again and again with a big knife until you have something that looks a bit like a salsa. It's a bit messy but it's totally worth it. Transfer to a bowl and season with the oil, lemon and salt and pepper.

Serve with the kofte and some nice bread.

Fried Pastries with Aubergines, Slow-cooked Lamb and Béchamel

Makes about 10 small pies

This is a dish that reminds me of moussaka when I eat it, but it's enclosed in a delicious olive-oil pastry. I love creating recipes with flavours that are familiar but you just can't pin them down. This is one of those and even though not found in Greece, Greek people love it.

For the lamb
- 50ml (2fl oz) extra virgin olive oil
- 400g (14oz) lamb shoulder off the bone, cut into bite-sized chunks
- 200g (7oz) red onion, finely diced
- 400g (14oz) fresh tomatoes, roughly chopped
- 200ml (7fl oz) red wine
- 1 cinnamon stick
- ½ tsp ground cloves
- ½ tsp ground black pepper
- Sea salt, to taste

For the pastry
- 400g (14oz) plain flour
- 200ml (7fl oz) olive oil
- 1 tsp vinegar
- 1 tsp sea salt
- Warm water (around 200ml/7fl oz)

For the béchamel
- 70g (2½oz) butter
- 1 tbsp plain flour
- 200ml (7fl oz) milk
- 150g (5½oz) hard sheep's cheese, grated

- 200ml (7fl oz) vegetable or olive oil for deep frying (use the same oil to fry first the aubergines and then the pies)
- 400g (14oz) aubergines, cut into thick slices and salted

Heat a saucepan over a medium heat, add the olive oil and brown the lamb all over. Add the onion, tomatoes, wine, spices and salt. Mix, adjusting the seasoning if necessary. Cover with a lid and cook for about 30 minutes or until the meat is tender and the sauce is thick. Set aside to cool.

To make the pastry, put the flour in a bowl and add the olive oil, vinegar and salt. Start adding the warm water slowly while kneading the dough. You usually need a similar amount to that of the olive oil. Stop adding water when your dough is soft and silky. Don't overknead the dough – stop as soon as you have a dough that is workable. Place in a bowl, cover with a damp cloth and let it rest for 15–20 minutes.

To make the béchamel, caramelize the butter in a small pan until it is golden. Add the flour and whisk vigorously for a minute. Add the milk and cheese and continue to whisk gently until the sauce thickens. Remove from the heat and set aside to cool.

Heat the oil in a pan until hot. Check the oil by lowering an aubergine into it – it should bubble instantly. Deep-fry the aubergine in batches until golden. Remove from the pan using a slotted spoon and drain them on kitchen paper to absorb the excess oil. Set aside to cool and reserve the oil in the pan.

To make the pies, roll out the pastry as thinly as you can without breaking it. Cut out rounds, about 10cm (4in), in diameter using a saucer.

In a bowl, mix together the lamb, aubergines and béchamel. Place about 1 tablespoon of the filling on one half of a pastry disc and fold over the other half to seal the pie and create a half-moon shape. Dip your finger in water and run it along the edges of the pastry then use a fork to seal the sides together. Fry the pies in hot oil until golden brown on both sides.

the MOUNTAINS

Slow-cooked Leg of Lamb with Orzo

Serves 4–6 as a sharing plate

This is a typical way of cooking lamb in Greece. What I love most about it is the aromas it releases as it cooks. It's one of those dishes that you know who is cooking it just by having a stroll through the neighbourhood.

Preheat the oven to 200°C/400°F/gas mark 6.

Heat the oil in a pan and brown the lamb gently on both sides. Add the garlic, juniper berries, rosemary, thyme and oregano and cook for a few more minutes until the garlic begins to colour. Add the tomatoes, black pepper and wine and cover the pan with a lid. Cook slowly for about 1 hour until the meat begins to become nice and tender. If you feel there isn't enough liquid in the pot, you can add some water.

Add the orzo and 200–300ml (7–10fl oz) water and adjust the seasoning. Transfer the contents to an ovenproof dish and cook in the oven for another 30 minutes. The dish should be juicy, but not watery, so it's very important that if you feel it needs extra water, you add this in small quantities. You want the sauce to emulsify and thicken and the orzo to be perfectly cooked. By this point the meat should be falling off the bone. Best served hot.

— 50ml (2fl oz) extra virgin olive oil
— 1 small leg of lamb (about 1–1.2kg/2lb 4oz–2lb 8oz), cut into 2cm (¾in) slices across the bone (ask your butcher to do this)
— 5 garlic cloves, roughly chopped
— 1 tsp juniper berries, whole
— 2 rosemary sprigs
— 2 thyme sprigs
— 1 tsp dried oregano
— 600g (1lb 5oz) ripe red tomatoes, roughly chopped
— 2 tsp freshly ground black pepper
— 500ml (18fl oz) good-quality red wine
— 250g (9oz) orzo pasta
— Sea salt, to taste

Lamb Cutlets with Lemon and Oregano

- 1kg (2lb 4oz) lamb cutlets

For the marinade
- 2 tbsp chopped thyme
- 2 tbsp chopped rosemary
- 1 tbsp dried oregano
- 6 anchovy fillets
- Zest and juice of 2 unwaxed lemons
- Zest and juice of 1 unwaxed orange
- 1 tbsp extra virgin olive oil
- Sea salt, to taste

Serves 4–6 as a sharing plate

In Crete, we are mad about lamb cutlets. Every taverna in the mountains has them and will argue that theirs are the best you've ever had. A lot of the taverna owners in the small mountain villages have their own animals and, needless to say, the meat they have on offer is incredible. You usually go into their eateries/homes and sit down at a table. No menu is available; the owner will come and say what he has – meat, salad, olive oil chips, wild greens and that's about it. A portion of meat is not really an option – they buy their cutlets by the kilo – so the taverna owner looks at the company around the table and quickly decides how many kilos you can manage. All that's needed is salt, pepper, oregano and a well-lit charcoal grill. The cutlets come to the table piping hot with lots of lemon halves. It may just be the best thing ever.

The marinade below strays away from the traditional simplicity a little but makes you want to eat these cutlets by the kilo – for sure!

Blitz all the marinade ingredients to a paste in a food processor. Put the cutlets in a dish and smother them with the paste. Place the dish in the fridge for at least 3 hours.

Light the barbecue and when the coals are red hot, cook the chops for a few minutes on each side. Make sure they don't catch fire when grilling, but if they do, just splash some water on the coals.

When cooked, take off the heat, transfer to a platter and enjoy with a nice fresh Cretan salad (see page 88). I also love serving the lamb cutlets with a spicy feta dip (see page 104).

Mutton and Spinach Rice with Goat's Butter

Serves 4–6 as a sharing plate

This is rich and hearty and so satisfying. Getting hold of goat's butter for this recipe is really worth it – it has a cheesy flavour and a savoury aroma that is simply unique and makes this rice truly delicious.

- 800g–1kg (1lb 12oz–2lb 4oz) mutton or leg of lamb, cut into slices on the bone (ask your butcher to do this)
- 100g (3½oz) goat's butter
- 200ml (7fl oz) white wine
- 1kg (2lb 4oz) spinach, washed and finely chopped
- 1 bunch of dill, finely chopped
- 1 bunch of mint leaves, finely chopped
- 150g (5½oz) short-grain rice
- 1 organic egg
- Juice of 4 lemons
- ½ tsp plain flour (optional)
- Sea salt and freshly ground pepper, to taste

Heat a pan over a medium heat and, when hot, add the mutton and the butter and brown gently on both sides. Season generously with salt and pepper, then add the wine and enough water to just cover the meat. Cover with a lid and cook gently for about 40 minutes. If you need to add more water, make sure you don't add too much as the spinach will also release water later on.

Put the spinach and herbs in a bowl, salt gently and massage for 1–2 minutes to release the aromas.

After 40 minutes, the mutton should be tender, but continue to cook if it needs longer. Add the rice to the pan, together with the spinach and herbs, and give everything a good stir. If there is not enough liquid to cook the rice, then add a touch more water. Cook for another 15–20 minutes until the rice is ready and the dish is juicy and creamy.

Whisk the egg in a bowl together with the lemon juice and flour. The flour is not absolutely necessary here, but it prevents the egg from splitting.

Remove the pan from the heat and pour in the egg mixture. Stir fast so the egg gets incorporated quickly and does not split. Return to a very low heat and stir for another few minutes until it all thickens a little. Check the seasoning and eat immediately.

You can reheat this dish but you will need to do it slowly and over a low heat. If you let it boil, the egg will split and even though the flavour will be the same, the texture will no longer be silky and velvety.

the MOUNTAINS

Cretan Phyllo Pies of Mutton and Wild Greens with Burnt Butter Yogurt

Makes about 10 small pies

Traditionally in Crete these are made as a large pie and usually with unboned mutton. The belief is that the meat is much tastier if the bones are kept intact and of course, eating becomes much more adventurous! After the meat has been boiled, the stock is used to make the dough, which adds richness. A combination of three Cretan cheeses makes it luxuriously rich. This version is simpler, delicious and maybe allows you to stand up from the table after dinner! The addition of a shot of raki to the dough helps make it crisper. A teaspoon of vinegar will do the same if no strong spirit is available.

This recipe uses wild greens. In the UK, you can use wild nettles, garlic leaves, sea spinach, chickweed, garlic mustard or wild fennel. If you can't get your hands on wild greens, use spinach, dill and chard in equal quantities.

For the phyllo pastry
- 400g (14oz) plain flour, plus extra for rolling
- 100ml (3½oz) extra virgin olive oil
- 1 tsp sea salt
- A shot of raki or grappa or 1 tsp vinegar
- 200–300ml (7–10fl oz) tepid water

- 2 tbsp extra virgin olive oil
- 1 white onion, chopped
- 200g (7oz) mutton, deboned and cut into walnut-sized pieces
- 100ml (3½fl oz) white wine
- 500g (1lb 2oz) wild greens, finely chopped
- 200g (7oz) Cretan mizithra or fresh goat's curd (or feta)
- 2 tbsp chopped dill
- 2 tbsp unsalted butter
- 100g (3½oz) Greek yogurt
- 200–300ml (7–10fl oz) olive oil or good vegetable oil, for frying
- Sea salt and freshly ground black pepper, to taste

For the pastry, put the flour in a bowl and add the olive oil, salt and raki. Make a well in the centre and start adding the water little by little. Knead until you have a lovely soft, silky, elastic dough. This dough does not need a lot of kneading so stop as soon as the right texture is achieved. Place a damp cloth over the dough and let it sit for 30 minutes or more.

Heat a small pan over a medium heat and add the olive oil with the onion and mutton. Season well with salt and pepper. Brown the mutton on all sides, add the wine and enough water to just cover the meat. Place a lid over the pan and gently cook the mutton until tender. This should take around 20–30 minutes. Remove from the pan and allow to cool, then shred the meat into a bowl. Add the chopped wild greens, goat's curd and dill to the bowl, season with salt and pepper and mix well.

Dust a work surface with flour and roll out the pastry as thinly as you can without it breaking. The thinner you get it, the lighter your pastries will be. Use a saucer, around 10cm (4in) in diameter, to cut out rounds and dust them with flour to avoid them sticking. Don't overdo it with the flour or you will change the texture of the pastry.

Take a tablespoon of the filling and place it in the centre of the disc. Fold over the disc to create a half-moon shape. Wet your finger with cold water and run it along the edge, then press gently to flatten the shape. Use the edge of a fork to seal the edges.

For the burnt butter yogurt, caramelize the butter in a pan over a medium heat until slightly darker than honey. Remove from the heat, stir in the yogurt and season with salt. Set aside.

Heat the oil in a frying pan over a medium heat. When it's hot (it should start bubbling as soon as a pastry is lowered into it), gently lower in the pastries and cook gently on both sides until golden. Remove from the pan and place on kitchen paper to absorb the excess oil. Serve with some burnt butter yogurt on the side and eat immediately. These are absolutely delicious cold too.

Beef Cheeks with Crushed Potatoes

Serves 4–6 as a sharing plate

Beef cheeks are great. They need to be cooked slowly and their flavour needs to be intense. At least, that's how I like them. This is one of those dishes that you want when it's cold outside and you have time for a nap after eating.

I have included orange wine in this recipe and, as I write this, I am smiling. Orange wine has become big recently and I must admit I like it – not all of it but most of it. I think the reason I like it is because it reminds me, in a way, of Cretan marouvas wine and Spanish dry sherry, both of which I love. I remember when I started working at Moro many years ago, the bar manager introduced me to Spanish sherry – I drank a small glass on my first shift as a waitress. I still remember the puzzlement inside me and, I assume, on my face as I was asked what I thought of it. I felt I knew this flavour, not as it was then and there, but it reminded me of something I knew well. What was it? I could not pin it down for ages. Time passed and I attended many Spanish sherry tastings in London and Spain. I still could not understand why I liked Spanish sherry so much and why, above all, I wanted it with food.

It was when I was in Crete on one of my family visits that it came to me. The sherry reminded me of the Cretan marouvas wine made from the red Romeiko grape we were brought up with. It's not red and it's not white, but something in betweeen; it's musty and aromatic and you order it by the kilo, not the litre. When orange wine started entering the scene in London, I indulged myself in it. What is this new creation that had most probably been resurrected from a very long time ago? The feeling was similar – the flavour, the lightness yet complexity and the mustiness – it all reminded me of Cretan wine.

These days, finding a bottle of orange wine or Spanish sherry is much easier than finding a bottle of Cretan marouvas, but if you are lucky enough to have the latter then of course use that.

- 2 beef cheeks (about 1kg/ 2lb 4oz)
- 150ml (¼ pint) extra virgin olive oil
- 2 large white onions, chopped
- 200g (7oz) pumpkin or squash, peeled and chopped
- 1 tsp ground allspice
- 1 tsp ground cinnamon
- 1 tsp freshly ground black pepper
- 1 tsp juniper berries, whole
- Zest and juice of 1 orange
- 200ml (7fl oz) orange wine or Spanish dry sherry, like fino
- 200ml (7fl oz) good-quality red wine

- 300g (10½oz) Cyprus potatoes, scrubbed
- 80g (2¾oz) mature hard cheese, grated (it's up to you what you use as long as it's powerful)
- Sea salt, to taste

Trim off any excess and hard fat from the beef cheeks and salt them. Place them in a single layer in a wide pan with 50ml (2fl oz) of the olive oil and sear them over a high heat until golden brown on both sides.

Turn down the heat to medium, add the chopped onions and pumpkin and cook for 10 minutes. Add the spices, orange zest and juice, wine and enough water to cover the meat by about 2cm (¾in). Lower the heat and cook extremely gently for about 4 hours. You want the meat to be soft like butter. Check that the seasoning is perfect before you take the pan off the heat. Allow to cool a little and break into smaller pieces.

Boil the potatoes in salted water. When cooked, drain in a colander and leave to steam dry. When they are cool enough to handle, but still hot, peel and mash roughly, then add the remaining olive oil, cheese and more salt if needed.

Serve with the beef cheeks and lots of the gravy. A bitter leaf salad seasoned with oil, salt and lemon goes perfectly here.

Slow-cooked Oxtail with Peppers and Olive Oil Chips

Serves 4–6 as a sharing plate

Oxtail is delicious but it's the olive oil chips that make this dish. I get funny looks when I say I cook my chips in olive oil, but this is quite standard in Crete and the chips taste different. The oil is drained after cooking and used again. In our family restaurant, we sold a lot of chips. We had turned a double fryer into a chip-only fryer and we always used olive oil. When we did this, our chip sales doubled and this came as no surprise. The flavour is irresistible.

— 4 red horn peppers
— 4 red chillies
— 3–4 leafy celery sticks
— 1.3kg (3lb) oxtail, cut into pieces
— 150ml (¼ pint) extra virgin olive oil
— 500ml (18fl oz) good-quality white wine
— 500ml (18fl oz) water
— Sea salt and freshly ground black pepper, to taste

For the olive oil chips
— 500g (1lb 2oz) Cyprus potatoes, washed and peeled
— 500ml (18fl oz) olive oil
— Sea salt, to taste

Char the peppers and chillies over the flame on a gas hob or in a frying pan placed over a high heat. You are basically using it like a hotplate. Blacken them all round, remove from the heat and trim and deseed them. Put them in a food processor together with the celery and blitz to a paste.

Heat a large saucepan over a medium heat. Season the oxtail with salt and pepper, add to the pan with the olive oil and brown on both sides. Add the wine to the pan together with the paste. Cook for 10–15 minutes and then add the water. Cover with a lid and cook very gently for about 3 hours. The time may vary, depending on the size of the pan and also on the intensity of your hob. It is cooked when the meat is so tender it falls off the bone when poked with a fork and the sauce is rich and sweet. Adjust the seasoning and turn off the heat.

When the oxtail is almost ready, cut the potatoes into thick discs and then across into chunky batons. Salt them generously and place them in a colander for 15–20 minutes. Heat the oil in a large pan. When the chips are added, the oil level will rise significantly so you need a big enough pan to allow for this in order not to create a dangerous overflow.

Drop in one chip to make sure the oil is hot – it should start bubbling immediately. Carefully lower all the chips into the oil and do not stir for at least 2–3 minutes. Give the chips a little stir to make sure they are all cooking evenly. Cook for about 10–15 minutes or until crunchy and golden on the outside and soft on the inside. Remove from the oil using a slotted spoon and place on a plate lined with kitchen paper to remove the excess oil. Eat immediately with the oxtail stew.

Beef with Dried Figs and Instant Pickled Salad

Serves 4–6 as a sharing plate

Figs complement this beef stew beautifully. They add texture and sweetness and give it a richness that satisfies the soul.

Heat a pan over a medium heat, add the butter, oil, orange peel and juniper berries and gently warm up for a minute or two. Season the meat with salt and pepper, add it to the pan and brown gently on all sides. Add the carrots and tomatoes to the pan together with 500ml (18fl oz) of water. Cover the pan with a lid and cook gently for 30 minutes. At this point the meat will still be tough.

Add the chopped figs to the pan and cover again with the lid. Cook for another 30 minutes and check whether the meat is now sweet and tender. It should break up when poked with a fork. During this process you may need to add extra water to the pan, but you want this stew to be juicy, not watery. By the time the meat is cooked, the sauce should be thick and emulsified.

While the beef is cooking, make the salad by slicing the cabbages very thinly using a mandolin and grating the carrot and kohlrabi using the coarse side of a box grater. Place everything on a board and roughly go over it with a knife to chop into smaller pieces. Put everything in a bowl, add the mint and fresh figs, then season with sugar, vinegar and salt.

Serve the beef in shallow bowls with the pickled salad on the side.

- 30g (1oz) unsalted butter
- 3 tbsp extra virgin olive oil
- Peel of ½ unwaxed orange
- 1 tsp ground juniper berries
- 700g (1lb 9oz) beef chuck or shank off the bone, cut into 8–10 pieces
- 200g (7oz) carrots, finely chopped
- 400g (14oz) tomatoes, roughly chopped
- 1 litre (1¾ pints) water, possibly more
- 200g (7oz) dried figs, rehydrated in hot water for 20 minutes and roughly chopped
- Sea salt and freshly ground black pepper, to taste

For the instant pickled salad
- ⅛ small white cabbage
- ¼ small red cabbage
- 1 carrot, peeled
- 1 kohlrabi, peeled
- 1 handful of fresh mint leaves, roughly chopped
- 2 fresh figs, peeled and diced
- 2 tbsp sugar
- 3–4 tbsp aged sweet white wine vinegar (depending on the intensity of vinegar)
- Sea salt, to taste

the MOUNTAINS

AEGEAN

Small Fried Pies with Pastourma, Cheese and Dill

Makes 10–15 pies

This is my favourite snack. I first had something similar in Turkey and thought it was incredible. Pastourma is an air-dried cured beef. As a child, the only person I knew who ate pastourma, and kept very thin slices of it in his fridge, was my Uncle Giorgos. He was a bit Italian, having lived there for a while, very funny and loved all things charcuterie. Having not eaten charcuterie much in Crete, I was completely oblivious to the fact that it is enjoyed in northern Greece in pastry, known as the 'pie from Caesaria' or Kayseri in Turkey. I tried it with my olive oil pastry and loved it even more. The combination of the not-so-strong melting cheese and the very intense flavour of the pastourma is perfect.

- 1 batch of olive oil pastry (see page 160)
- 400g (14oz) mild melting cheese (a mild Cheddar works perfectly here), cut into short thick slices
- 15–20 slices of beef pastourma (you can find this in Turkish shops, often called pastirma)
- 1 bunch of dill, finely chopped
- 200g (7oz) tomatoes, finely chopped
- Sea salt and lots of freshly ground black pepper, to taste
- 200–300ml (7–10fl oz) vegetable oil, for frying

Make the dough as described on page 160. Roll out the pastry quite thinly on a floured surface and cut it into roughly 8cm (3¼in) squares. Add some cheese and pastourma to each square, followed by a little dill and a few bits of tomato. Season with salt and lots of black pepper.

Dip your finger in cold water and run it over the edges of the square. Grab two opposite corners and bring them to the centre, then pinch them together. Do the same with the remaining two corners and then, using your fingertips, pinch together the open sides to seal the whole pastry.

Heat the oil until hot but not smoking. Check by lowering a pie into the oil – it should bubble instantly. Fry the pies in batches until golden and the cheese has melted. Remove from the pan and drain on kitchen paper. Eat warm.

Ox Tongue with Caper and Lemon Butter

- 1–1.2kg (2lb 4oz–2lb 8oz) ox tongue
- 1 large onion, quartered
- 1 ripe red tomato, chopped
- 1 kiwi fruit, peeled and chopped
- 1 tsp chilli powder
- 1 tsp cinnamon
- 1 tsp ground nutmeg
- 3 cloves
- 4 large sage leaves
- 300ml (½ pint) white wine
- 50g (1¾oz) orzo pasta

For the caper and lemon butter
- 50g (1¾oz) unsalted butter
- Juice of 2 lemons, plus extra for dressing
- 2 tbsp capers
- 1 tsp chilli flakes
- 2 anchovy fillets
- A few lemon thyme sprigs, leaves stripped from the stems
- Sea salt, to taste (you may not need this)

- Extra virgin olive oil, for dressing
- Red radicchio leaves to serve and some sourdough bread
- Sea salt and freshly ground black pepper, to taste

Serves 4–6 as a sharing plate

Alex, my husband, loves ox tongue. I'd never really had it, but when we went to his home town of Veroia in the north of Greece, we visited a small eatery for lunch and enjoyed it sliced thinly with lots of black pepper and olive oil. It was so good that I wanted to try and include it in my cooking more, because I wanted to experiment and also to cook something he really craves. Of course I could not just boil it in water alone, so I have added a whole load of aromatics and the secret ingredient – the kiwi. The acid in the kiwi fruit is usually used in the marinades of tough meats to help tenderize them and here it's included in the boiling bouquet to do the same job.

Wash the tongue well under cold water and place in a pot with with all the other ingredients. Add enough water to cover it and more – remember that you are boiling the tongue, not making a stew. Bring to the boil, lower the heat to simmering and cook gently for 3–4 hours until the tongue is tender and a fork penetrates it with ease. You will need to top up the water sporadically to keep the tongue well covered. When the tongue is ready, season generously with salt.

I have to mention that the following instructions were not my intention. My idea for this dish was to chill the tongue, slice it the next day, put lots of black pepper on it and serve it with the butter, salad leaves and hot bread.

It was very late one night when I cooked this and Alex came back from work asking me what the amazing smell was. When I said it was tongue, he was very happy and opened the pot to try the broth. He got a bowl and served himself some broth. I jealously copied him. It's one of the best meat broths I have ever tried. Therefore, I now suggest that you remove the tongue from the broth and place it in the fridge to chill and then you add 50g (1¾oz) of orzo pasta to the pot and cook until ready. Serve the broth first, followed by the tongue salad.

Make the butter by blitzing it in a food processor with the lemon juice, capers, chilli flakes, anchovies and lemon thyme.

Serve the tongue, thinly sliced and dressed with olive oil, lemon juice, salt and black pepper. Warm up some thinly cut slices of sourdough and put the butter on the side. I like to have some red radicchio leaves on the plate, too.

AEGEAN

Crispy Filo, Custard and Cretan Mangoes

Serves 4

Depending on the season, you can change the fruit in this dessert. In autumn, I love roasting plums with a touch of sugar and a splash of water and pouring them on top.

— 3 tbsp melted butter
— 6 sheets filo pastry
— 1 tbsp caster sugar

For the custard
— 400ml (14fl oz) double cream
— 200ml (7fl oz) whole milk
— 2 cardamom pods, seeds
  removed and crushed
— 6 egg yolks
— 100g (3½oz) caster sugar
— 1 tsp fine semolina

— 3 fragrant mangoes
— Juice of 1 lemon

Preheat the oven to 160°C/325°F/gas mark 3.

To make the custard, put the cream, milk and cardamom in a pan and bring to a gentle boil. Lower the heat to minimum and let it simmer while you whisk the egg yolks. Using an electric mixer, whisk the yolks with the sugar and semolina until pale and creamy. Take the cream off the heat and, quickly, whisk in the egg mix. Return to the heat while whisking continuously on the lowest setting for another few minutes or until the custard thickens. Transfer to a dish and chill in the fridge.

Place a sheet of pastry on a small baking tray and brush generously with some of the melted butter followed by a sprinkle of sugar. Place another sheet on top and brush with more butter and a sprinkling of sugar. Repeat this until all six sheets are layered on top of one another in the tray. Score the pastry with a sharp knife into squares or diamonds. This will allow air to enter the pastry and it will puff up in the oven.

Cook in the oven for 20–25 minutes or until golden brown. You want all the layers to be golden and crispy, so check the bottom layers before you take it out of the oven; if they are not crispy, turn them upside down and cook for a little longer. It does not matter if the pastry breaks up a little as this is what you will end up doing to it anyway. Remove from the oven, place on a rack and allow it to cool down.

How you prepare the mangoes is up to you. If you want texture, you can remove both sides of mango flesh from the stone, score them and use as the little skinless cubes or you can scoop all the flesh out to end up with bigger chunks. You could also make a purée by blitzing it. Mix the mango with the lemon juice and let it sit.

To serve, break some golden filo on a plate, pour over some custard and then the juicy mango. Other soft fruit, like strawberries, raspberries and peaches, are also delicious here.

Semolina Cake with Syrup

- 300g (10½oz) plain flour
- 3½ tsp baking powder
- A pinch of sea salt
- 180g (6¼oz) semolina
- 50g (1¾oz) ground almonds
- 6 organic eggs, separated
- 200g (7oz) caster sugar
- 340g (11¾oz) unsalted butter, cut into cubes
- Zest of 2 unwaxed oranges
- Seeds from 1 vanilla pod
- 250ml (9fl oz) orange juice

For the syrup
- 600g (1lb 5oz) caster sugar
- 500ml (18fl oz) water
- 1 tsp ground cinnamon
- 2 tsp brandy

The quantities below make quite a big cake but it keeps well.

In Greece, you find many cakes made with semolina – some without flour and others with both flour and semolina; some with yogurt, others with milk; some flavoured with gum mastic and others with oranges and lemons. This is an old recipe with a few tweaks. I have added ground almonds and freshly squeezed orange juice, which make it very aromatic. It's super easy to put together and lasts in perfect condition for a good few days.

Preheat the oven to 180°C/350°F/gas mark 4. Line a 24x30cm (9½x12in) cake tin with baking parchment (or use a bundt tin if you have one).

Sift the flour, baking powder and salt into a large bowl and add the semolina and ground almonds.

Using an electric mixer, beat the egg whites until frothy, add half of the sugar and continue beating for a couple of minutes, until soft peaks form.

In a separate bowl, beat the yolks with the remaining sugar and the butter until creamy and pale. Add the orange zest, vanilla seeds and orange juice to the egg yolks and then add the dry ingredients. Mix well using a wooden spoon. Fold in the egg whites until the mixture is well blended. Pour into the cake tin and cook in the oven for about 45–55 minutes or until the cake is golden and a knife inserted into it comes out clean. Remove from the oven but leave in the tin.

Make the syrup by boiling all the ingredients together for 10 minutes. Pour the hot syrup over the cooled cake – you will need to do this slowly as it will not take the syrup in one go. To make this process easier, you can poke holes into the cake with a cocktail stick to help the absorption of the syrup.

This is delicious with some ice cream, some yogurt or simply as it is.

the AFTERS

Orange and Broken Filo Pastry Pie

Serves 4

This is a cake I had heard about many times and attempted to make a few times too, but with no luck. It was not until I went to the south of Chania to Sougia, a magical place with a rocky beach and ice-cold waters, that I was offered it again after many years. It was a friend's mum who made it and it was divine. It was light and fluffy and melted in your mouth. Nothing like my heavy and stodgy attempts of the past. Using filo pastry instead of flour creates these amazing layers in the cake and texturally it becomes something else, something new. The syrup then soaks everything and as it's not heavy and thick, the cake remains light and airy. She gave me her recipe.

— 1 pack (500g/1lb 2oz) baklava filo pastry

For the cake
— 250g (9oz) caster sugar
— 250g (9oz) Greek yogurt
— 250ml (9fl oz) rapeseed oil
— 5 organic eggs
— Zest of 2 unwaxed oranges
— 1 tbsp baking powder

For the syrup
— 500g (1lb 2oz) caster sugar
— 200ml (7fl oz) fresh orange juice
— 500ml (18fl oz) water
— 1 cinnamon stick
— 2 cardamom pods
— Zest of 1 unwaxed orange

— A few fresh bay leaves (optional)

Preheat the oven to 140°C/275°F/gas mark 1. Lightly butter a 20cm (8in) round cake tin.

Cut the filo pastry into thin strips and place on a baking tray. Dry in the oven for about 20 minutes or until crisp. Increase the oven temperature to 160°C/325°F/gas mark 3.

Whisk all the cake ingredients together in a bowl, preferably using an electric mixer, for a couple of minutes.

When the filo is dry enough, add it to the cake mixture and mix with a wooden spoon. Pour into the cake tin and cook for about 45 minutes–1 hour, until it is golden and a knife comes out of the cake clean.

While the cake is cooking, make the syrup. Place all the syrup ingredients in a pan, bring to the boil and continue cooking for another 5 minutes. Set aside and allow to cool.

When the cake comes out the oven, remove the cinnamon and cardamom pods from the lukewarm syrup and pour it over the cake. You may need to make some holes on the surface of the cake with a cocktail stick to allow the syrup to soak in.

I like to serve this cake with bay leaf dust. Blitz a few fresh bay leaves in a spice grinder or food processor then rub through a fine sieve to get a bright green dust that will really complement the orange aromas and looks fabulous too.

AEGEAN

Buttery Biscuits with Lemon Cream and Fresh Strawberries

Makes 15–20 biscuits

These are delicious. The crunchy buttery biscuits with the tangy lemon cream and the sweet fruit is one of my favourite combinations. I like to serve the biscuits whole on the side so I have spoonfuls of the cream and fruit and then a mouthful of the biscuit. If you prefer you can crumble the biscuits over the top and then have it all with a spoon.

For the biscuits
— 110g (3¾oz) butter, softened
— 50g (1¾oz) brown sugar
— 50g (1¾oz) fine semolina
— 125g (4½oz) plain flour
— 4 green cardamom pods, seeds removed and crushed to a fine powder

For the lemon cream
— 100g (3½oz) cream cheese
— 100g (3½oz) Greek yogurt
— 70ml (2½fl oz) double cream
— Juice of 2 lemons
— 100g (3½oz) caster sugar

— 300g (10½oz) fresh, fragrant strawberries
— 30g (1oz) caster sugar
— 1 tbsp rosewater
— 100g (3½oz) shelled unsalted pistachio nuts, crushed
— 1 tbsp icing sugar, to dust (optional)

For the biscuits, cream the butter and sugar together. Fold in the semolina, flour and cardamom powder. Mix and form into a dough. Shape the dough into a square, wrap in clingfilm and place in the fridge for a couple of hours. This will help to stop the dough from crumbling too much.

Preheat the oven to 180°C/350°F/gas mark 4. Line a baking tray with baking parchment.

Using a sharp knife, cut the dough into rectangular shapes about 0.5cm (¼in) thick and place on the lined tray. Bake for 15–20 minutes. Remove from the oven and set aside.

For the lemon cream, put all the ingredients in a mixing bowl and whisk gently until smooth and silky. You can do this with an electric mixer or with a hand whisk.

Hull and cut the strawberries into quarters and put in a bowl with the sugar and rosewater, then stir. Let them sit for 15–20 minutes.

To serve, place a generous tablespoon of the cream on a plate, followed by the macerated strawberries and the crushed pistachios. Finish with a biscuit or two on the side and a dusting of icing sugar, if you like.

Loukoumades with Honey, Cinnamon and Sesame

Makes 20–30, depending on size

We grew up with loukoumades. In Greece the saints have name days and the churches associated with the saint whose name day it is have massive celebrations with gigantic feasts laid out on tables taking over whole village squares. These are called 'panigiria'. This is where you often see the ladies cooking tons of loukoumades. They have the most amazingly fast technique where they force the batter through their thumb and index finger and use a spoon or their other hand to pinch it off and drop it into the hot oil. They are so fast you can hardly follow. It seems that they make hundreds in minutes – and most probably they do.

These are very easy to make and even more satisfying to eat. The secret is to eat them immediately; don't let them sit or they will go soggy.

— 240ml (8½fl oz) tepid water
— 7g (1 sachet) dried yeast
— 1 tbsp caster sugar
— 200g (7oz) plain flour, sifted
— 1 litre (1¾ pints) vegetable oil, for frying

For the syrup
— 170g (6oz) honey
— 120ml (3¾fl oz) water
— ½ tsp ground cinnamon
— 1 strip lemon peel
— 2 strips orange peel

To decorate
— 2 tbsp sesame seeds
— 1 tbsp runny honey

Put the water, yeast and sugar in a bowl and add the flour slowly while mixing the batter with your hands. Cover the bowl with a tea towel and put to one side until it doubles in size and you can see bubbles in the batter.

Heat the oil in a large pan over a medium heat. Check the oil is ready by adding a bit of batter – it should bubble instantly.

Place the syrup ingredients in a small pot and bring just to the boil. Remove from the heat and put to one side. Take a tablespoon of the batter and gently drop it into the hot oil using another tablespoon to scrape the batter off the first. It sounds trickier than it is – the batter is quite sticky so it doesn't just drop off the spoon, you will need to help it using the second spoon. Keep wetting your spoons in cold water to make it easier. The batter will initially sink to the bottom, but within seconds float to the top. You need to stir the balls gently so all sides turn golden and crispy, at which point remove them from the pan using a slotted spoon and place on kitchen paper to absorb the excess oil.

Toss them in the hot syrup and place on a platter. Scatter the sesame seeds all over and drizzle the extra honey. If you'd like them to be extra syrupy and sweet, you can add the leftover syrup to the platter, too.

the AFTERS

Almond and Raisin Pastries with Carob Molasses

AEGEAN

For the pastry
— 300g (10½oz) plain flour
— 50g (1¾oz) polenta
— ¼ tsp ground allspice
— ½ tsp ground cinnamon
— 180g (6¼oz) salted butter, softened
— 2 tbsp caster sugar
— 50ml (2fl oz) milk

For the filling
— 200g (7oz) raisins
— 200g (7oz) raw almonds
— 1 tsp ground cinnamon
— 5 tbsp carob molasses (grape or date molasses also work here)

Makes 10–15 pastries

I remember my godfather shouting my name from the bottom of the stairs and calling me to come down as we were going for 'chocolates'. I don't think I ever went for actual chocolates with him. Instead he would lift me and flip me onto his shoulders and we would head into the fields. He was tall and moved fast and I felt I was on top of the world. I didn't have to worry about jaggy bushes or stinging nettles getting my legs; I just had to balance a bit and enjoy the view from above. We would go past the well and the small animal farm and countless olive trees. We would go past the caves, and he would tell me about how people hid in these during the war and then we would arrive at the 'chocolate shop' – the carob tree. I knew which ones were ready to eat as they would be dripping with sugary syrup and I would behave like a wild goat on his shoulders in order to get where I wanted. One in each hand, a few in my pockets and off we went back towards the house. I love to use carob in its natural form – making my own flour and my own molasses. These pastries are exactly how I like my sweets. They are not too sweet, they are crunchy and buttery and with a hint of chocolate coming from the carob.

Preheat the oven to 170°C/325°F/gas mark 3.

Put all the pastry ingredients in a bowl and bring together to form a soft dough. Wrap it in baking parchment and put to one side. Don't refrigerate it as you want the dough to be malleable.

For the filling, blitz the raisins and almonds in a food processor until fine and transfer to a bowl. Add the cinnamon and carob molasses and give it a good mix.

Line an oven tray with baking parchment and tear off a piece of dough the size of a walnut. Flatten it on your palm to cover most of it and then take a smaller ball of the filling and put it in the centre. Bring all sides of the disc up to enclose the filling and shape it into a ball, then flatten it a bit and place on the baking tray. Repeat until dough and filling are used up. Bake in the oven for about 30–40 minutes until the pastries are light and golden.

Tahini Cake with Metaxa Brandy and Sweet Samos Wine Butter Sauce

Serves 4

This is one of my favourite cakes. The tahini keeps it moist and the sweet wine sauce gives it a richness that makes you go back for more and more. It's easy to make and keeps for days.

Preheat the oven to 180°C/350°F/gas mark 4 and oil a 900g (2lb) loaf tin.

Using an electric mixer, whisk the tahini, orange juice and icing sugar until smooth and pale. Transfer to a bowl and fold in the flour and baking powder until the mix looks evenly combined. Add the raisins and orange zest with a pinch of salt and mix once more.

Mix the sesame seeds with the caster sugar. Scatter the sesame-sugar mix all over the base of the tin and pour the cake mix on top. Cook in the oven for about 45 minutes or until the surface looks crunchy and golden and a pointed knife comes out clean. Remove from the oven and turn out onto a rack to cool.

Make the butter by putting the brandy, sweet wine and sugar into a pan over a medium heat and reducing it by two-thirds. Turn the heat down as low as possible and whisk in the chilled butter little by little. By the time all the butter has been added, the sauce should be thick, glossy and delicious.

Serve slices of the cake with some of the rich sauce poured over the top.

— 150g (5½oz) tahini
— Zest and juice of 2 unwaxed oranges
— 200g (7oz) icing sugar
— 190g (6½oz) plain flour, sifted
— 15g (½oz) baking powder
— 130g (4¾oz) raisins
— A pinch of sea salt
— 1 tbsp sesame seeds
— 25g (1oz) caster sugar
— 1 tsp extra virgin olive oil, for greasing

For the butter sauce
— 50ml (2fl oz) metaxa (or another decent brandy)
— 100ml (3½fl oz) Samos sweet white wine (or similar)
— 2 tsp caster sugar
— 100–120g (3½–4oz) unsalted butter, chilled and cut into cubes

the AFTERS

Rose Turkish Delight Ice Cream

— 300ml (½ pint) double cream

— 300ml (½ pint) milk

— Seeds from 4 cardamom pods

— 100g (3½oz) caster sugar, plus 1 tsp

— 3 organic egg yolks

— 200g (7oz) rose-scented Turkish delight, finely chopped

Makes about 10 servings

When I was small I hated the smell of rosewater. 'It smells like grannies!' I used to say whenever I was offered something flavoured with it. Thinking back, I wasn't that wrong as the grannies I knew smelled of either rose or another very particular lemon scent from a perfume called Myrto. It took a while for me to use rosewater and appreciate its contribution to dishes. It actually happened when I started working at Moro with Sam and Sam Clark. They used rosewater in ways I could have never imagined and made savoury sauces, ice creams and scented creams and lots of other amazing things. I still don't use it as much as I want to but despite my initial feelings regarding grannies and roses, I often find myself mixing it with olive oil to clean my skin after a hard day's work in the kitchen.

I came across some very nice Turkish delight, another sweet I have never been very keen on, and thought I would try to turn it into ice cream. I was more interested in the texture and whether the jelly-like sugary cubes would add something new. Well, I made it and it was delicious and I have to stop myself from making it too often as I end up on the sofa with a spoon and the whole tub.

Put the cream and milk in a heavy-based pan over a medium heat. Crush the cardamom seeds with 1 teaspoon of sugar in a pestle and mortar and add to the milk and cream. Beat the egg yolks with the remaining sugar using a whisk or an electric mixer until pale.

When the milk and cream come to the boil remove from the heat, add the egg and sugar mix while whisking continuously. Return to a low heat and cook for a few minutes while stirring until the mix thickens and resembles custard. Transfer to another chilled container and allow to cool for a bit before adding the Turkish delight. Put in the freezer for a couple of hours and bring it out to give it a good whisk; repeat once more and allow it to freeze undisturbed after that until the desired texture is achieved. If it hardens too much then let it sit out of the freezer for a while before serving.

Angel Hair Filo with Gum Mastic Ice Cream and Sour Cherry Preserve

Makes about 10 servings

Gum mastic ice cream and sour cherries are so good together. I think it's a combination going back to my childhood where the hundreds of small kiosks dotted around, known as 'periptera', sold a version of this. I still remember the tub, which was midnight blue with a female figure dressed in dark pink and with quite an intense look. It came in small cups and in family-size tubs. My dad used to always send me to buy a big tub for the house, as he loved it, but I never actually remember it getting to our freezer. We all got a spoon each and gathered around the tub taking massive spoonfuls and scoffing it down at great speed. It was pure white, light and creamy and laced with a delicious sour cherry syrup. Here, the addition of angel hair filo adds a crunch and makes it a more complete and satisfying dessert.

For the filo
— 150–200g (5½–7oz) angel hair filo (found in Greek and Turkish shops)
— 80g (3oz) unsalted butter, melted
— 4 tsp caster sugar

For the mastic ice cream
— 300ml (½ pint) double cream
— 300ml (½ pint) milk
— 3g (¹⁄₁₆oz) gum mastic granules, crushed into a powder with 1 tsp sugar
— 1 cardamom pod, seeds removed and crushed
— 3 organic egg yolks
— 100g (3½oz) caster sugar

For the sour cherry preserve
— 200g (7oz) frozen sour cherries
— 100g (3½oz) caster sugar
— Zest and juice of 1 unwaxed lemon

Preheat the oven to 160°C/350°F/gas mark 3.

'Untangle' the angel hair filo, rub the butter into it and sprinkle the sugar all over. Spread out on an oven tray and bake for about 20 minutes or until it's golden and crispy. Remove from the oven, let it cool and store in an airtight container until needed.

To make the ice cream, put the cream, milk, powdered gum mastic and cardamom seeds in a pan and gently bring to the boil, then remove from the heat. In another bowl, beat the egg yolks and sugar until pale and add them to the cream mix while whisking continuously. Return the pan to a low heat and continue to stir until the mix thickens and resembles custard. Churn using an ice cream maker, if you have one, and freeze. (Otherwise, allow the mix to cool, then pour into a freezerproof dish and beat using an electric hand mixer twice; first after 2 hours in the freezer and then again after 1 hour. Let it freeze until desired consistency is achieved.)

For the preserve, cook the cherries with the sugar over a medium heat for about 20 minutes. Turn the heat off and add the lemon zest and juice. Let it cool down before using.

To serve, place some angel hair filo at the bottom of a plate or bowl and add the ice cream followed by the cherry preserve.

Pastelia – Sesame and Nut Bars, Dipped in Dark Chocolate

Makes 20–30

Pastelia are found everywhere in Greece and all around the Eastern Mediterranean in various shapes and forms. They are usually made with peanuts, almonds, pistachios and often just with sesame. Most of them are hard like brittle as they are made with sugar. This recipe is more like an energy booster. It's packed with seeds and fruits and nuts and is sweetened only with honey. It is actually a healthier version and I can't wait to give them to my son, Ermis, to munch on.

— 300g (10½oz) good-quality honey
— 150g (5½oz) walnuts
— 200g (7oz) raw almonds
— 100g (3½oz) pumpkin seeds
— 100g (3½oz) raisins
— 100g (3½oz) sesame seeds
— 1 tsp ground cinnamon
— 150g (5½oz) good-quality dark chocolate
— 2 cardamom pods, seeds removed and crushed
— Zest of 1 orange

Heat the honey very gently in a pan until it becomes liquid, but don't let it boil.

Put the walnuts, almonds and pumpkin seeds in a dry pan over a medium heat and toast gently for a few minutes. Transfer to a food processor, add the raisins and roughly blitz.

Add the sesame seeds to the hot honey followed by the nut mix and the cinnamon. Return to the heat and give everything a good stir. Use a spatula to take off any mix stuck to the sides of the pan. Remove from the heat and allow to cool enough to handle.

Line a tray with baking parchment. Wet your hands and pick up walnut-sized pieces of the mix. Roll into balls, slightly flatten with your thumb and place on the tray. Allow to sit for a few hours to dry out a little. They will never go hard as they don't contain sugar. The honey helps keep them soft and chewy.

Melt the dark chocolate and cardamom in a bowl set over a pan of simmering water.

When the chocolate is melted and glossy, remove from the heat, add the orange zest and allow to cool a bit. Dip the pastelia, one by one, in the chocolate, return to the tray and allow the chocolate to harden. If you want, you can add a touch of tahini or brandy to the melted chocolate.

Apple, Peach and Almond Tart with Sweet Yogurt

Serves 4

This is easy, familiar and everyone loves it. The ground almonds in the pastry and the peaches are the reasons I crave this so often. If you feel like something sweeter, serve it with vanilla ice cream instead of yogurt.

— 250g (9oz) butter, cut into cubes and chilled
— 250g (9oz) self-raising flour
— 125g (4½oz) ground almonds
— 125g (4½oz) muscovado sugar
— 2 red apples, cored, peeled and cut into 2cm (¾in) cubes
— 2 ripe peaches, stoned, peeled and cut into 2cm cubes
— 85g (3oz) caster sugar
— 50g (1¾oz) flaked almonds

For the sweet yogurt
— 200g (7oz) Greek yogurt
— 50g (1¾oz) icing sugar
— Zest of 1 orange
— ½ tsp ground cinnamon

Preheat the oven to 180°C/350°F/gas mark 4. I usually use a 20cm (8in) square ovenproof dish, but anything of a similar size will work.

Put the butter, flour, ground almonds and muscovado sugar in a bowl and rub with your fingertips to make fine crumbs. This may take a while but it's quite a good 'time out' activity.

Press two-thirds of the crumb mixture into the dish. Mix the apples, peaches and caster sugar in a bowl and wait for the sugar to dissolve — it won't take long, about 10 minutes. Pour this over the crumb mix and scatter the remaining crumbs over the top followed by the flaked almonds. Cook in the oven for about 45 minutes–1 hour until you can smell the sweet aroma and the top is golden and crunchy.

Mix the yogurt with the icing sugar, orange zest and cinnamon and serve alongside the tart.

the AFTERS

Hung Yogurt with Baked Peaches and Toasted Almonds

- 300g (10½oz) Greek strained yogurt
- 8 tbsp caster sugar
- 2 cardamom pods, seeds removed and crushed
- 1 tsp ground cinnamon
- 4 ripe peaches, halved and stoned
- 3 tbsp water
- 50g (1¾oz) flaked almonds
- 1 tbsp thyme honey

Serves 4–6 as a sharing plate

In our restaurant in Crete we never had a dessert menu. Actually, I think most places I go to don't offer one. This does not mean that you can't have something sweet after your meal, it simply means that it's an offering and you will get whatever the cook has decided. We used to send out platters of fresh fruit and Greek yogurt with seasonal preserves. Our most popular preserve was carrot. It surprised most people when they asked what that delicious bright orange preserve was and learned it was carrot. Nobody expected that a vegetable could be transformed in such a way. We would also make sultana grape preserve, quince and bergamot, orange and cherry – whatever we fancied really. And that was it: fresh fruit, yogurt with syrupy preserves and a cold bottle of tsikoudia (Cretan raki) to aid digestion, of course. Some would argue that this sounds more like a breakfast plate than a dessert but I think it's my favourite end to a meal. It's fresh, light and not too sweet; it is the Greek palate cleanser.

Mix the yogurt in a bowl with 4 tablespoons of the sugar, cardamom and cinnamon. Line another bowl with a cheesecloth or another clean cloth and pour the yogurt mix in. Make sure the cloth is big enough to allow you to bring the sides together and tie a knot with a piece of string just above the mix. Hang overnight with a bowl underneath to collect the dripping liquid. The next day, take the mix out of the cloth and put aside. It should have thickened so it resembles cream cheese. You can discard the liquid – you don't need this.

Preheat the oven to 180°C/350°F/gas mark 4.

Put the peaches in a tray with the remaining 4 tablespoons of sugar and the water and bake for about 20–30 minutes. You don't want them to go mushy so keep an eye on them.

Place the flaked almonds in a dry pan over a medium heat and toast gently until they begin to colour at the edges.

To serve, put dollops of the strained yogurt on a plate followed by some peaches and top with flaked almonds and a drizzle of honey.

Sesame, Chocolate and Tahini Biscuits with Greek Coffee

— 250g (9oz) plain flour
— A pinch of salt
— 2½ tsp baking powder
— 100g (3½oz) tahini
— 100g (3½oz) caster sugar
— 2 medium organic eggs
— 1 tsp vanilla extract
— 50g (1¾oz) dark chocolate (70% cocoa solids), chopped into small pieces
— 60g (2¼oz) sesame seeds
— 40g (1½oz) caster sugar

For the Greek coffee
— 200ml (7fl oz) cold water
— 2 heaped tsp Greek coffee
— 1½ tsp sugar

Makes about 20 biscuits and 2 small coffees

These biscuits are slightly salty and not too sweet. Adding the chocolate just makes them more luxurious and so moreish. I love having them with Greek coffee, which I explain how to make below; however, any good quality coffee is suitable. The small pot used to make Greek coffee is called a 'briki' and you can find tiny ones that hold enough liquid for just one coffee or slightly bigger ones for making more. As the sugar needs to be added at the beginning, I usually make mine medium-sweet and cross my fingers that everyone will be happy.

If you don't have a 'briki', make sure you use the smallest pot you own with the smallest opening. This will help get a creamy top on your coffee, called 'kaimaki', which is very important!

Preheat the oven to 160ºC/325ºF/gas mark 3.

Sift the flour, salt and baking powder into a bowl. In another bowl, beat the tahini and sugar together until creamy, then add the eggs gradually while beating.

Add the vanilla and continue to beat until pale and creamy. Fold in the dry ingredients until everything is just combined and a uniform dough has formed. Mix in the chocolate pieces.

Mix the sesame seeds and sugar together in a bowl. Take small, walnut-sized bits of the dough and roll them between your palms to form balls. Flatten slightly and roll in the sesame seeds and sugar. Place on a baking tray lined with baking parchment and bake for 15 minutes or until they have hardened a little on the outside and are golden. The biscuits may be a touch soft when you check them, but they will firm up as they cool.

To make the coffee, add the water, coffee and sugar to the pot or 'briki'. Place on a hob on the lowest setting possible and give the contents a stir. Patience is required as the slower the coffee is made, the better it will be. Wait for a couple of minutes and give the coffee one final stir. Now wait again, but don't leave the coffee. In a couple of minutes you will see the coffee puffing up, starting from the sides and going towards the centre. It looks like a ring slowly closing. As the ring closes, take the coffee off the heat and pour it into 2 small cups. If a nice creamy layer forms on top then you have made a good one!

the AFTERS

Bougatsa – Sweet and Salty Cheese Pastry with Sugar

— 500ml (18fl oz) milk
— 2 tbsp semolina
— 5 tbsp caster sugar
— 200g (7oz) feta, crumbled
— 230g (8oz) mizithra (Cretan goat's curd) or another good-quality soft goat's cheese, crumbled
— 120g (4¼oz) butter, melted
— 250g (9oz/½ standard pack) filo pastry (more or less)
— Caster sugar, for sprinkling

Serves 4–6 as a sharing plate

In the centre of Chania is Bougatsa Iordanis. This traditional eatery has been run by the same family since 1924 and the only thing served is freshly made, crispy, sweet and salty bougatsa. It opens its doors really early to catch the before-work and late-night work souls. Admittedly, I have also been there at the crack of dawn, but usually after a long night partying rather than a hard night's shift. Every time I go to Chania, I stop and have a portion of bougatsa. As you enter the space, there is a heavy seriousness in the air that makes it feel almost sacred and like you have to behave and be quiet. You sit at one of the tables and the lady that has been there since I can remember comes to you with a glass of water and an authoritarian aura. You give her your order, she nods and goes to the counter, where the bougatsa is kept in a big glass display. The required amount is chopped off, weighed, sprinkled with sugar and slid onto a plate. That's it – simple, delicious, traditional and full of history. This is my version, as the original recipe is a secret.

Preheat the oven to 170°C/325°F/gas mark 3. Line a large baking tray with baking parchment.

Put the milk, semolina and sugar in a pan and slowly bring to the boil. Whisk occasionally to make sure the semolina doesn't stick together in a clump. After about 10 minutes the mix will begin to thicken; at this point add the feta and goat's curd or cheese to the pan and whisk gently so everything comes together. Continue cooking over a low heat until the thickness resembles that of thick double cream and turn the heat off. Allow the mixture to cool, place in a bowl and refrigerate for at least 1 hour or until it becomes very thick.

Open the pack of pastry and unfold it so each sheet is flat and all are stacked on top of each other. Cut it in half lengthways and store one half in the fridge wrapped in a damp cloth. (You may use it for something else or you can double the filling recipe and make lots of bougatsa and freeze them.) Cut the remaining pastry sheets in half again lengthways. Take two sheets, brush with some butter, then place a tablespoon of mix at the bottom allowing a 1cm (½in) gap from the end of the pastry nearest you. Take the bottom right corner and fold it over to cover the filling and meet the other end. Fold the covered half again to meet the opposite side and create a triangle shape. Continue doing this all the way to the top until you have used all of the pastry. Dip your fingers in water and pinch the sides of the triangle to make sure they are well sealed. Repeat with the remaining pastry and filling. Place the triangles on the tray and brush with some of the leftover butter. Bake for about 25 minutes or until golden and crispy on the outside. Remove from the oven and place on a board. Cut them into bite-sized pieces and sprinkle with as much or as little sugar as you fancy.

Cheese Fritters with Honey

Makes 10–12

I was so happy the first time I made these. My initial thought was for them to be served as a dessert but then we put them on the menu at Morito Hackney as a starter and people loved them. My favourite comment regarding these came from a Greek customer who came up to the pass and said, 'Those fritters! Oh my god; they taste like the pies from the village of Sfakia in Crete.' I hadn't made the connection before this but he was right. They closely resemble the famous 'Sfakianes pites' – very thin round pastries enclosing Cretan goat's curd and pan-fried in hardly any oil and then drizzled with lots of thyme honey. They are usually eaten after a hearty meal in the mountains and always with a shot of tsikoudia (Cretan raki). Even though these fritters are very different, the flavour you get from them takes you to the same place. They are perfect for breakfast, lunch and dinner and, of course, as an 'after' too.

- 1 red onion, diced finely
- 1 tbsp extra virgin olive oil
- 200g (7oz) feta
- 200g (7oz) soft goat's cheese or Cretan mizithra (goat's curd)
- 1 small bunch of fresh mint leaves, chopped
- 2 organic eggs
- 1 tbsp plain flour
- 2 tbsp white sesame seeds
- 2 tbsp black sesame seeds
- 2 tbsp plain flour
- 1 litre (1¾ pints) vegetable oil, for frying
- 2–3 tbsp thyme honey, for drizzling

Put the onion in a small pan with the oil and cook gently until sweet and translucent. Set aside to cool.

Crumble the feta and goat's cheese in a bowl and add the onion, mint, eggs and flour. Mix well until everything is combined. Place in the fridge for 30–40 minutes to firm up.

Put the sesame seeds and flour on a plate.

Take 1 tablespoon of the cheese mix in your hands. Roll into a ball and then toss in the sesame-flour mix. Repeat until all the mixture is used up.

Heat the oil in a pan over medium heat. Check that it is hot enough by dropping in a tiny bit of the cheese mix – the oil should immediately start bubbling around it.

Lower the cheese fritters gently into the hot oil and cook until golden and crispy on all sides. Remove from the oil using a slotted spoon and place on kitchen paper for a few seconds to absorb the excess oil.

Serve with thyme honey drizzled all over. Eat immediately.

Mountain Tea with Graviera

Serves 4

The pairing of Graviera and mountain tea goes back a long way. I remember my granny offering it to me almost every time I visited her and she encouraged me to finish it as it would protect me from winter colds. She would often put a small rusk next to a thick slice of Graviera and sometimes dunked it in her tea like a biscuit to soften it up a little. She would put lots of thyme honey in the tea and often pour a bit over the cheese; this too would prevent me from catching any colds.

These days I choose to source mature Graviera that has been ageing for about a year and the texture is firmer and the flavour more intense. In Crete, it's traditionally made from 100% sheep's milk but in other areas of Greece, cow's milk as well as goat's is used. Graviera ripens for a minimum of five months before it is put up for sale and the final product varies a lot depending on the producer. The fact that the animals are free to roam and graze the rich flora of the island ensures a beautifully flavoured cheese that is very popular.

The mountain tea mostly used in Crete, called malotira, is a shrub with fluffy pale green leaves and yellow flowers. It grows all around the mountainous areas of the island and especially in the White Mountains near Chania. It is widely known for its medicinal properties and is often used together with other herbs like sage, oregano, pennyroyal and marjoram, all with additional therapeutic properties.

Whether used on its own or with other herbs, this tea is so comforting, aromatic and full of only good things. The addition of honey adds to the aromas and gives it the perfect touch of sweetness. If you prefer it cold, then chill it and serve it over ice with a slice of lemon.

Put a handful of malotira in a teapot or jug and pour boiling water over it until the pot is full. If you want to add other herbs then add teaspoons of them as you want the main flavour to come from the malotira. Also, too much oregano or sage, for example, will make the tea too strong.

Allow the tea to sit for 10 minutes and serve it with as much or as little honey as you like, wedges of Graviera and Cretan barley rusks (paksimadia).

Index

UK/US GLOSSARY

aubergine – eggplant
baking powder/bicarbonate of soda – baking soda
baking tray – baking sheet
beetroot – beet
biscuit – cookie
clingfilm – plastic wrap
chips – fries
coriander – cilantro
courgette – zucchini
double cream – heavy cream
frying pan – skillet
grill – broil/broiler
icing sugar – confectioners' sugar
jam – jelly
mince – ground meat
prawns – shrimp
plain flour – all-purpose flour
rapeseed oil – canola oil
rocket – arugula
self-raising flour – self-rising flour
starter – appetizer

Acknowledgements

I want to thank Alexandros, my partner who helped me enormously throughout this project and has been truly amazing. He has supported me and encouraged me every step of the way. He ran, he drove, he cooked, he gave me ideas and above all he was there. To many more projects together. I love you.

I would like to thank my whole family for supporting me so much during the writing of this book, in so many ways I can't even begin to describe. I want to thank my dad Lyssandros for taking us fishing, running around fish markets and harbours and being so happy to help in every way possible; for being so patient with photographs and so willing to chat to everyone that crossed his path for this book. My brother Antonis who has been so proud of me and ran around to make sure things were proper and perfect and my sister Kimberly who put up with all of us again and again.

My friends in Greece and England who have been so excited and have helped me from the beginning to the end. My best friends Anneta and Matina in Crete who have just been the best people to call when immediate help is needed and always sort everything out for me.

Big thanks to Brendon and the team at Finn and Flounder on Broadway market. They managed to satisfy my very picky needs regarding fish throughout my experimenting and testing for this book.

Thanks to Maltby & Greek, who have provided me with amazing Greek products for the past few years and put up with lots of phone calls and peculiar home deliveries while testing recipes for this book. Without a doubt they are passionate about their work and have consistently provided me with exquisite Greek and Cretan products.

A big thank you to Blenheim Forge who provided me with some amazing handmade knives to work with throughout this adventure.

Thank you to the Trikalinos family in Greece that make the best bottarga I have ever tried and generously sent me lots of amazing things to try and experiment with.

A big thank you to Manousakis winery near Chania, who were amazing and very welcoming when we visited and spent time cooking and tasting their beautiful wines. Their approach to making wine is honourable and they work with respect towards nature and passion to ensure that their wines reflect the rich soils of the island.

Massive thanks to Kallergi refuge in the White Mountains in Crete and to the amazing people running it all year round. We cooked and shot dishes at 1,680 meters altitude surrounded by breathtaking mountain peaks and a fully equipped kitchen!

Thanks to Chatzivarity winery in Greece for introducing me to their delicious wines and their great achievements with natural wines. They are outstanding.

I have a very big thank you to say to all the team at Octopus/Kyle Books for all their hard work and endless support, especially Sophie Allen who was there the whole time and dealt with everything with tremendous calm and professionalism.

My photographer and friend Elena Heatherwick who understands me and shares my feelings and made this book really feel special. She captures people and situations in the most honest way and makes the simple act of looking at a picture generate more emotion and excitement than one can possibly imagine. Thank you.

A big thank you to Charlie Brotherstone, my agent who a way back was introduced to me and went for it. I truly appreciate everything you have done.

Thanks to Eleanor Mulligan for being a star throughout our trip to Crete and our hectic schedules. Her help in the kitchen was invaluable.

Finally I want to thank Ermis, my son who, only months old, was extremely patient and amazing and allowed me to test and retest endless recipes in our kitchen. We laughed and sang and tasted lots and he was incredible. I love you.